We Want The World

Jim Morrison, The Living Theatre and the FBI

by Daveth Milton

BENNION
KEARNY

Published in 2012 by Bennion Kearny Limited.

ISBN: 978-0-9570511-8-8

Published by Bennion Kearny Limited
6 Victory House, 64 Trafalgar Road
Birmingham, B13 8BU

www.BennionKearny.com

Cover image: ©Tischenko Irina

About the Author

Daveth Milton is a critic and scholar who writes on popular culture.

About the Book

The events portrayed in this book are based on the real-life events of Jim Morrison and The Doors between 1969 and 1971. However, a degree of dramatic license has been taken when 'recreating' certain events including the Flight to Phoenix and Jim's engagement with The Living Theatre - so readers are advised to treat the work in the manner to which it was intended – inspired by the true story.

Foreword

Reaching Out For the Dawn

Prison. Confinement. Incarceration.

Up to three years of nothing, but four walls, for a victimless crime that maybe he didn't commit. That was the prospect facing - contradicting - Jim Morrison, main lyricist and lead singer for The Doors. Who could imagine that the man who lived so free could be reduced to a number in Florida's penal system?

The FBI keeps over five and a half million pages of surveillance information in their Washington archive. Jim Morrison's dossier consists of just ninety-two. But don't worry. It would be wrong to equate the size of his file with the significance of his opposition. The Bureau deals with only a fraction of all crimes, and their archive contains no information on a rebel like James Dean and only 4 pages on Jerry Garcia of the Grateful Dead. For public figures that did come under FBI scrutiny, the important question is: *what really happened?*

Bureau agents pursued two main cases against Morrison. I was lucky enough to obtain the material they accumulated. Despite its presentation (in sterile government prose) and condition (almost Xeroxed into oblivion), Morrison's file contains interesting secrets. It suggests a new story; a story showing that the FBI's infamous director, J. Edgar Hoover, knew all about Jim. The file also highlights the importance of the time when Jim Morrison indulged in drunken revelry on a flight to Phoenix in November 1969. Over two thirds of the dossier is about that incident, yet it never appeared in Oliver Stone's 1991 film *The Doors*. As Jim's lover, the writer Patricia Kennealy, put it in her book *Strange Days*, '*…there was probably a REAL conspiracy going on - the FBI really was out to get Jim Morrison - and Oliver let it get right by him.*' [1]

So did Kennealy. The Phoenix incident only got four lines out of 573 pages in *Strange Days*. Pointing out such an important omission is not a case of fault-finding, as her account aims only to detail her life with Jim. Nevertheless it pinpoints a continuing critical silence - an untold story.

In an early press release Jim explained, '*I've always been attracted to ideas that were about revolt against authority. When you make peace with authority, you become an authority. I like ideas about breaking away or overthrowing of established order. It seems to be the road toward freedom.*' [2]

How could the Establishment not pursue a man who began his public life with a mission statement like that? To the Bureau's director, Morrison was more than a criminal - he represented a different way of life. Consequently, Jim Morrison and the FBI had a hostile meeting of minds.

What was the size and shape of their awkward encounter? Together with biographical evidence, Jim's FBI file guardedly suggests Hoover and Morrison were important to each other. In his memoir *Light My Fire*, Doors' keyboard maestro Ray Manzarek explained, '*It was definitely 'us against them'. The lovers, artists, and poets against the powers of the Establishment.*' [3]

So, looking through the government dossier, I knew that what I had in my hands was a metaphysical thriller.

What do I mean by metaphysical? I mean that although Hoover and Morrison never actually met, at one of the most taut moments in twentieth century history, they became engaged in a kind of long-distance mutual antagonism. The pair pursued diametrically opposed projects. Both claimed to be protecting freedom. Each blocked the other. And yet, even though each man knew his opponent only through scraps of evidence, phantoms and mind-pictures, nothing short of America's future hung in the balance.

You want the real Jim Morrison? His public life appeared turbulent and rebellious. Ray Manzarek told journalists, '*It was an act, man. Boris Karloff wasn't Frankenstein, you know.*' [4]

But although I have based this book on the truth as far as I know it, I would add a word of caution. At least in the early days, for Jim Morrison easy separations between art and life did not exist: there is good evidence for deciding that the man initially preferred his myth. Jim couldn't say his occupation when a film maker asked him as he was stepping off a plane in 1968. He didn't have a 'job', only a life. Insofar that he could control it, his image was the message he was trying to convey. By acting out interviews, rejecting his family, inventing his background and slowly forging his persona, he grew into a self-made man-mystery. Mysteries require effort from us to make sense of them.

Perhaps it would clarify matters to approach the singer through his actions. What was the nature of Jim's mission? To say he made a loving critique of America is only one part of the story: the journey, not the goal. According to Patricia Kennealy, Jim once described himself as: '*an actor-musician-dancer-politician... writer... Well, politician only in the broadest sense.*' [5]

From Morrison's surreal UCLA movie to *The End* (the song), The Ed Sullivan Show to New Haven, Miami to Phoenix, Morrison's career lurched forward in a series of shocks. His critics saw him as a tragic and self-destructive star, but they themselves may have been misguided. Was Jim not aiming to be part of an instructive tradition? Many of those shocks were, after all, premeditated. The Doors lead singer is remembered for his tendency to confront society's restrictions.

Jim Morrison struggled toward the dawn.

From the beat poets, Jim took the idea that society granted poets a special life of license and abandon: rebellious intoxication, a derangement of the senses. Morrison was interested in reporting from altered states. He lived out his art because he needed his risks to be real, not just for the sake of his own experience - he always aimed to inspire.

According to William Blake, '*The road of excess leads to the palace of wisdom.*' [6] Jim did not lead by dictation, or even by example. Instead he literally stayed on the edge as a way to serve his own brutal curiosity about life. He charted out humanity's options by exploring its extremes.

Peddling their fascinatingly robust mixture of teen dreams and ancient nightmares, The Doors set a precedent in rock by scaring their audiences. Jim's words made the music because they were the electric sparks that gave rise to a sound so ageless and moody that it frightened people. Jim proved over and over that nobody could tell him what to do. When the band first practiced, its singer announced the end of Western civilization. As Ray said, they were involved in a slow '*dismantling of the military-government-industrial-complex.*' [7]

Although he remains one of rock's most compelling and authoritative voices, Morrison was essentially an interloper who seized the power of music to propagate his own unusual aims. By constantly reaching for the most appropriate characters, questions and metaphors, Jim Morrison tried to free us all from the simpleminded, voluntary and often unconscious ways we relinquish control of our lives to other people. As he told Lizze

James in 1967, '*How can I set anyone free who doesn't have the guts to stand up and declare his own freedom?*' [8]

Jim unlearned his fears so he could embrace dangerous new liberties of thought, expression and being. He wanted to open up doors between controllable art and insane life, between our shadowy society and personal inner darkness. He told Ray, '*We have to take people inside themselves. Those places they're afraid to go into.*' [9]

Human beings fail to live life to the fullest because they fear their own feelings. There came a band in response, a band that Ray Manzarek called '*possessed patriots of freedom*'; their Nietzschean creed being that if we have the courage - reach out and grasp, destiny is ours to control.[10]

Perhaps Morrison's biggest mistake lay in believing that so many would want to go with him. Others soon realized the menace of The Doors' musical concoction. A&R men and Los Angeles club owners had one word for that music: 'Sick!'

And then there were always officers of the law: those little men in blue suits who halted one of the band's early rehearsals at Hank's place in LA. They broke up Elektra's party at the Delmonico Hotel in 1967 after a punch-drunk Jim declared himself in charge of proceedings. They shut down The Shrine nightclub just when The Doors were playing. They arrested John Densmore for vagrancy because he walked around with long hair. And they made Jim the first rock singer ever to get arrested on stage, in New Haven. As Densmore said, soon The Doors '*were becoming notorious as a radical group.*'[11] The FBI was just around the corner.

An early indication of the impending showdown between Morrison and Hoover happened when another freedom fighter - Martin Luther King - crossed swords with the Bureau's aging director. The FBI began to hound King for daring to speak up about civil rights. Hoover's biographer Anthony Summers called it '*the most vicious character assassination*' that the director had ever orchestrated.[12]

Agents tried to steer King away from picking up his Nobel Peace Prize. They implied he might commit suicide as a public favour. Fortunately, the Reverend King was strong enough to continue his quest, despite such harassment. But on April 4th 1968 he died in Memphis, aged thirty-nine - assassinated by a sniper's bullet. The Doors had only just released the single *Unknown Soldier.*

Martin Luther King's death shattered the civil rights movement and left a nation in shock. Fires, riots and other disturbances filled the void that followed in over a hundred cities. Thrown by King's death, Jim told his friend Linda Ashcroft that he felt America was losing her conscience. He took up the theme in poems like American Prayer, which provided his country with a rather unconventional reminder: she was founded on liberty, not on persecution.

Increasingly Jim's critique became a product of his own personal experience. His friend Robert Glover felt so harassed by the authorities that he declined an invitation to join The Doors on their 1968 European tour. Glover thought that Morrison: '*could do more with a crowd of people than the US government and Frank Sinatra combined...* [After raids on the Black Panthers] *The Jim Morrison I knew realized he might soon become Number One on the Establishment's hit list.*' [13]

Interest in the life of Jim Morrison continues unabated, encouraged by his legacy of over one hundred songs and dark, romantic poetry. What follows is not a full biography, but an interpretive sketch of his final two and a half years. Instead of focussing solely on Jim's artistic and personal life, my mission is to convey the desperation of the poet-singer who tangled with Hoover and his agents. I have set this against the volatile politics and urgent cultural response of late '60s America - a time when the country had lost her conscience.

The first chapter sets the scene, explores Jim Morrison's interest in The Living Theatre and shows how much he drew on their techniques during his desperate show at Miami's Dinner Key auditorium. Subsequently, I reveal Jim's designation as an FBI fugitive, suggesting that the repercussions of that fateful evening spread far and wide. After that, the Bureau had it in for Morrison. Then I examine their efforts after the madness on-board Continental Airlines Flight 172 to Phoenix and the surprizing legal result. Finally comes Morrison's long-awaited Miami trial, his bid for freedom, and his flight to Paris.

I'm not trying to exculpate Jim Morrison from his folly. I suspect he might have done things differently with hindsight. Who wouldn't? But that is hardly the point. The reality of Morrison's desperate performance in Miami had little to do with his indictment. Jim's violation of moral taboo came at a sensitive time and struck sparks on a tinderbox of major social tensions. Almost inevitably the shaman then became a martyr: a healer upon whom others could project their own hang-ups.

Forces in power decided that Morrison should take the punishment (more a rite than a cure) for the changes they refused to confront. According to Dostoevsky in *Diary of a Writer*, '*It is not by confining one's neighbour that one is convinced of one's sanity.*'[14] Nevertheless, Jim Morrison's case became a conspiracy of the ill-informed against the ill prepared - a circus. The story is a bold example of what Morrison discovered and Hoover already knew: justice is only incidental to law and order.

My aim is to celebrate Jim's challenge to those people who deployed the judicial machine without neutrality as a way to prevent the disappearance of a society they had always known. The Doors' poet-singer pushed hard against others' ruling ideas in order to live a new way of life, even at the risk of his own death. He had little choice, because experience was his inspiration - and he conveyed his emergent philosophy in a burning language of light.

Thankfully, Jim's legacy of art and example still allows us to question - and find independence from - our future in a world made for us. His songs and story remain an inspirational conduit to the other side of night.

J. Edgar Hoover thrived on repression, Jim Morrison on liberation. Although both are long dead, we still await the dawn.

1
Strange Days

A slow smile played across the singer's face.

He scratched his beard - he was pleased to help.

Twenty-five hundred dollars.

Toying with a phone he'd pleaded into beforehand, the tall man at the desk was visibly relieved.

Chapter 1

Julian Beck found himself at the noose end of a long day. New York was uncommitted, but his performance commune The Living Theatre really needed the money. And of all people! Here was Jim Morrison, like a duck out of water in San Francisco, offering to help - offering twenty-five hundred dollars. Just think: Jim Morrison - the great American showman, the ultimate face of criminal and sexual intent - buying into revolution…

Sunday March 9th 1969. Promoters had cancelled The Doors' planned Jacksonville gig. Accompanied by beat poet Michael McClure and his wife Joanna, Morrison went AWOL and tailed Beck up to the psychedelic city.

Radical, experimental theatre troupe The Living Theatre were expecting to perform in Golden Gate Park that afternoon, but after being set up by a pro-violence leaflet they cautiously arrived two hours too late. Now, as the afternoon shadows drew across City Lights' book publisher Lawrence Ferlinghetti's office on the Haight, Jim poured out superlatives. Julian Beck and his partner Judith Malina, and both the McClures, listened with heads bowed.

Beck and Malina were an odd couple. Julian had haunting blue eyes, withered brows and a generous mouth. He darted across the room trailing his halo of straggly, grey hair like a kind of amiably camp old teacher - expressive, sprightly, remonstrating. Before an audience Julian Beck could seem almost too much. With friends he appeared more restrained and remote; awkward even. His wife Judith Malina was warmer, less didactic and more animated. She was a much smaller person with penetrating black eyes - big eyes, always rimmed with mascara - eyes that could command a room full of people without difficulty. Judith was slightly scatty, slightly gypsy, but always politically committed.

Between them the couple took an unconventional approach to theatre. They wanted *reality* on stage: action, struggle, commitment. In fact, they learned a lot about acting - true *performance* (a whole behaviour learned in front of the audience) -

from another activity: jazz, especially the honking frenzy of musicians playing the smoky clubs in New York City. Beck and Malina lived theatre, politics, and their own commune with remarkable sincerity. They never divided life into little pieces.

Julian never voted because it meant leasing your power to someone else who told you what to do. The couple squarely opposed the entire system of Western government. Accordingly they avoided official theatre buildings as they did not want the art of theatre to be the property of the State.

Although they convened their New York-based troupe in the late '40s, the couple first hit the headlines in 1964 with a production called *The Brig*. Written by an ex-marine, *The Brig* was a tale of terror set in a prison: the army's special punishment block for disobedient soldiers. The Living Theatre's hatred for military coercion was spelled out in the play, in the same way that The Doors spelled out theirs in *Unknown Soldier* and *American Prayer*.

Malina used the marines' own handbook to put her cast through a relentless schedule of rehearsals. Going for realism had drawbacks - at least one actor suffered a nervous breakdown – but that just reinforced the point. The company wanted to purge society of war by displaying an unwatchable shred of sanctioned violence: burn the fingers as a reminder to put out the fire.

The Living Theatre's production of *The Brig* emerged in difficult circumstances. Julian Beck remained a persistent dreamer. His theatre company was insolvent again. They owed New York State and the IRS over $30,000 in back-taxes so Beck perpetually scratched around just to make ends meet. His city creditors may have turned a blind eye to anyone else, but The Living Theatre had organized annual General Strikes across America. Their new production expressed such uncompromisingly tight politics that it began to get everybody's back up. How could the authorities ignore performers who were trying so hard to question the system? The tax debt was a weak point.

Chapter 1

The IRS closed The Living Theatre's Fourteenth Street building in October 1963, but the company refused to leave. Since they believed their tax bill was not justified, Julian and the gang staged a sit-in and looked out from a second floor office window while a crowd gathered below. Judith Malina observed, '*We were more or less besieged inside the theatre... The streets were full of people chanting in our favour beyond the police line.*' [1]

At the end of the week they performed a special last production of *The Brig* - now a protest play in the midst of a protest. Police removed the actors by force and prosecuted them on eleven counts of 'interfering with Federal Officers.' Beck and Malina responded by turning their trial into a joke - chanting in the courtroom, and messing around as the prosecutor tried to limit the couple to legal procedures. Although the couple received small jail sentences for contempt of court, the media loved it.

After sitting-in, getting arrested, and colourfully subverting their own trial, in September of 1964 The Living Theatre's core membership left America to begin a new phase: travelling as nomads throughout Europe. To their surprise, they found society slowly catching up with them: revolution was in the air. So the troupe settled briefly at the Villagio Magico in Sicily early in 1968 and planned a new venture called *Paradise Now.*

Impossible to describe, amazing and intimidating to see, *Paradise Now* was not so much a play as a *fire*: a euphoric panic, spreading out of control from the theatre into the streets. The performance was visionary in all senses. Beck and Malina came into their own as cultural leaders, peddling a potent brand of magic realism and conveying their anarchist message.

The *Paradise Now* piece was an open text, a continual group-improvisation: a ladder of rites, visions and symbols, ascending from daily life into revolution. It was crazy. A question. A thrill. Just fun – yet also a deadly serious game: a way to take people out of themselves.

The *Paradise Now* evening revolved around a framework that included thoughts, expressions and challenges. Players enacted scenarios of conflict, simulating events in Paris, New York, Alabama and Cape Town. The troupe saw it as non-fiction acting. They moved toward utopia; not through bloodshed, but by giving the spectators a taste of what *could* be. During the first rehearsal Malina argued, '*For me it can't be political enough... In Paradise, reality changes.*' [2]

All Living Theatre performances became delirious freak-outs with stomping beats, screams, collective humming and swaying, but *Paradise Now* was an even more direct piece of social dynamite. Barriers were broken; lives re-made. At the Sports Palast in Berlin the whole atmosphere resembled an immense rock gig. Every message was drilled in by repetition: lots of shouting and screaming. Big theatrical statements. *Paradise Now* became several hours of exhausting human contact – always radical and sometimes intimidating. Standing close to their spectators, fuzzy naked hippies yelled, '*I'm going to flip out every day to blow your mind... That is the struggle!*' [3]

Even the diminutive Judith could roar like a female wrestler on stage. Members of the audience would touch the actors. Human bodies drew themselves into grotesque shapes. Faces beamed while hands held burning banknotes. The atmosphere was electric.

The cast was diverse, a multi-cultural assemblage of young radicals. Each performance began with actors dispersed through the theatre, repeatedly chanting, '*I am not allowed to travel without a passport... I don't know how to stop wars... You can't live if you don't have money... I am not allowed to smoke marijuana... I am not allowed to take my clothes off!*' [4]

Upon the last challenge, the troupe crossed a line. They began undressing and encouraging others to join in. Everyone who was bold enough would go naked in an act of political protest.

During the second 'rung,' the troupe made use of their acrobatic prowess. From the centre came a voice,

'Where are you? How long will you live?

What do you want?'

'I am here. It is time to revolt, to be free,' the actors replied.

'What is this called?'

In small teams, each creating a letter with their joined-up bodies, the actors spelled out ANARCHISM.

'What is anarchism?'

The letters changed to PARADISE and the company shouted, 'NOW!'[5]

True to their word, The Living Theatre's explosion went way beyond auditorium buildings and into the street. Beck and Malina took *Paradise Now* to Paris, London, Rome and Madrid. Touring through France the troupe got involved in the 'events' of Paris (May '68) when students from Nanterre occupied the Odeon and the Sorbonne. Next they arrived at the Avignon Festival, where local organizers refused them permission to stage the play.

If changing society meant a long climb up the ladder, it began with each individual's revolutionary consciousness. May '68 proved that some people already had the necessary feeling. Around two thousand kids had asked to join the troupe since it left America. Some followed the performances around for days. Judith and Julian suggested people should set up their own companies. Soon, eleven active spin-off troupes toured the European theatre circuit. The time was right to bring their message back to the States. As Judith Malina said, '*When we left America* [in 1964] *everyone thought it was a kind of humorous exaggeration when we said in answer to questions about theatre's aims: "To bring about revolution." Now this word is on everyone's tongue.*' [6]

Julian would stridently march around and proclaim, '*None of us is free until we're all free. All or nothing. Utopia. Paradise Now! Love is perfection.*'[7] He was also aware of the obstacles. His troupe understood that the revolution had not happened yet and that they were opposed by something much bigger, working non-stop to prevent change and to keep a different system in control.

The pinnacle of that something was the FBI: law enforcement *as* politics by another means. With offices in five foreign capital cities in 1968 the Bureau stood tall as a law enforcement agency of over 14,000 men. It specialized in monitoring and suppressing any activity that aimed to undermine America. Operating in secret, this 'Big Brother' organization tracked The Living Theatre's Volkswagen train on its way through France. An agent in Paris reported Julian's revolutionary statements back to Washington. To the white knights of America, Beck appeared an Undesirable. He led a ragged band of hippies and proclaimed a message that poured acid on the mainspring of society: its next generation.

Having decided to return to America, Beck and Malina opted for a six-month visit. The troupe would go on a tour organized by Saul Gottlieb's Radical Theatre Repertory. But the return to their native land was dogged by a sense of foreboding. Judith Malina recorded the panic of cast-member Jenny Hecht in her diary. Hecht sat on the floor crying, she said, '*I read the* [tarot] *cards: We are in danger. We are in danger of falling under the power of a great king.*' [8]

Judith explained, '*She is expressing everyone's paranoia. She says we're going to America to get killed.*' [9]

Later Jenny said that she had seen a vision of Julian, assassinated.

When they arrived in New York at the end of August, one reporter warned that America wasn't ready for them. Behind the public controversy there was also a private crisis. It would be easy for US authorities to eject a group they saw as political agitators simply by using non-payment of taxes as an excuse. So accountant Rubin Gorewitz asked Julian to sign a compromise pact with the government over the outstanding tax bill. Beck's refusal to sign forced everyone to live in constant danger, but The Living Theatre stood firm. Beck and Malina had survived their baptism of fire over *The Brig*. Four years later, they planned to survive again. But before reaching San Francisco the troupe were busted.

When *Paradise Now* was a success, it ended with the scantily-clad crowd rushing into the street and voicing spontaneous shouts of revolutionary joy. Late in September 1968, New Haven police called that indecent exposure, breach of the peace, and resisting arrest. Less than three weeks after they set foot on American soil again, the troupe were in serious trouble.

Five members of the cast and five spectators from the Yale theatre spent a night in the cells without beds, wearing only their *Paradise* garb. Since he had dropped out of Yale a quarter of a century earlier, Julian felt a strange sense of homecoming. In court he reluctantly claimed his G-string was a theatrical costume. As Malina noted, the local papers were now full of weird stories about nude men chasing nude women out of the theatre. Just over a week later, a judge fined Judith and her friend Ira Cohen $100 each for interfering with an officer.

And that was only their *first* US performance of *Paradise Now*. In November Boston's Hancock Hall blacklisted the troupe, so they played at the Roxbury ghetto instead. Julian got arrested again, this time within the YMCA theatre. His wrists were lacerated by the handcuffs. Later, busted a third time, he got a small fine in Philadelphia for:

> *'... one of those smaller technical charges. Obstructing an officer, or breach of the peace, or one of those no-crimes crimes which exist to justify the police; so that it doesn't look as though the cops bust people, especially artists and names-in-the-paper-image people for nothing.'* [10]

Paradise Now was cancelled or busted for making noise in the street, for indecent exposure, for breach of the peace, for too many people inside or outside the theatre. Local authorities were uneasy: '*None of the officials will say they don't want a play that advocates anarchism.*' [11]

Hounded, blacklisted, arrested and abused - the company faced ever-mounting odds. Money was tight. Gottlieb the promoter hadn't delivered everything he promised. On the bright side, Ted Mann made a generous offer to install the troupe at the Henry Miller Theatre on Broadway. If the Living Theatre had been almost any other company, it might have secured everything they could have wished for: stability, acceptance and a strategic new platform. Remembering the trouble over *The Brig*, Julian refused the offer. He decided not to sell-out and the troupe kept going. Beck even declined a $4,000 donation put forward by an enthusiastic disciple. Some of the cast were starting to get pretty angry about his judgement.

Meanwhile, except for the *Village Voice*, critics never seemed to get it. Whoever heard of actors being so difficult with their audience? Why did nobody laugh? How could the Living Theatre call upon *our* humanity when *theirs* was so clearly missing? To the critics *Paradise Now* was simply bad theatre.

Besides, the play appeared a bit naive. Out-for-blood radicals thought you had to fight for anything worth winning: the idea of a revolution without violence was simply an illusion. Julian, on the other hand, remained adamant.

Chapter 1

As The Living Theatre trekked across the Mid-West, members went down with the flu and other minor infections. They had broken-even on previous shows, but as audiences began to dwindle, the money got tighter and tighter. As the tour continued, it was heading for financial disaster.

2
A Glimpse of Paradise

In about the middle of December '68, down on Santa Monica Boulevard, Jim Morrison was slumped in a chair with his feet up, reading November's edition of the west coast activist magazine *Ramparts*. Life had been bugging him lately. I mean, what a year!

On the face of it The Doors were a real success; the only new rock group on the brink of playing New York's Madison Square Garden. Yet Jim still felt troubled, ill at ease about his country's predicament. Martin Luther King had been shot dead in Memphis, the Tet Offensive had come to light in Vietnam, kids had been stomped outside the Democratic convention in Chicago, and another Kennedy was dead and gone. America had become sucked deeper into a whirlpool of pain and Nixon, complete with his special brand of Republicanism, was installed in the White House.

What had Jim done? Talked of revolt, and of freedom. But what was he *known* for? *Light My Fire* and *Hello I Love You.* And here, on the pages of *Ramparts*, was a middle-aged anarchist named

Julian Beck being interviewed about his own controversial antics, explaining, *'When you're an anarchist, you're interested in the greatest amount of change possible.'* [1] A couple of months later Jim got the chance to see what Julian Beck might mean…

As The Living Theatre's still-battered Volkswagen train approached the west coast, late in February 1969, Judith Malina got a strange and uneasy feeling. In her diary she noted, *'Everything in California is very loaded, as in a dream, when a certain scene seems deeply significant but you don't know why.'* [2]

American kids were either seeking violent pathways to revolution or they didn't care at all. As the home of Flower Power, California was almost too liberal for *Paradise Now.* Instead of rapping against the State, students made love, smoked dope in their bedrooms, and listened to records. Some of them liked The Doors. Nevertheless, for one week only The Living Theatre brought their plays - culminating in *Paradise Now* - to the University of Southern California.

Although his fellow Doors never attended the show, Jim went together with a small group of friends which included Michael McClure and the band's young, blond Canadian manager, Bill Siddons. Morrison bought tickets for all the shows and took The Living Theatre's advance-man Mark Amitin out to dinner. Just as the North Vietnamese launched a major offensive against one hundred cities, over in California there was a meeting of minds.

On Monday the 24th of February 1969, The Living Theatre performed *Mysteries and Smaller Pieces*: a harrowing collection of scenes ending in the gruesome enactment of Antonin Artaud's idea, the *Plague.*

Artaud was amazing. As a man on the margin between normality and insanity, he lived his whole life disconcerted by the drama of his own body. He refused the division between mind and matter, just as he refused almost every other loyalty on offer - religion, family, logic, you name it. His ideas left an indelible mark on theatre, but his real value was as the maker of poetic metaphors.

And the most significant of these, which came in the midst of his collection *The Theatre and Its Double*, was *Plague.*

Plague heralded a new reality. For Artaud, theatre could transcend fiction and become life - not *acting* but *action.* He used taboo images (death, incest and scandal) to SHOCK audience members into an infectious madness.

Plague, in Artaud's schema, was a violent and overwhelming crisis with the power to transform a growing number of individuals and eventually all society. The disease became an ordeal helping people to break on through to the other side. They would emerge from it either purged or dead.

The Living Theatre loved Artaud. Even before they knew him, they followed a parallel course and tried to wake up spectators. Judith Malina claimed that the feeling of being taken from a theatrical *Brig* prison into a real one: '…*was an Artaudian experience that I think we've used within our work.*' [3]

When Mary Richardson completed an English translation of *The Theatre and Its Double*, Beck and Malina were amongst the first to know. By this time Artaud was long dead, but in Paris the Becks befriended his old companion Jean Barrault. Barrault addressed a speech to The Living Theatre when everybody occupied the Odeon. During May '68, the students who occupied the Latin Quarter distributed Artaud's *Letter to University Chancellors* in which he said society had mummified itself under the chains of frontiers, factories, law courts and universities. Through the revolutionary spirit, it was as if Artaud's plea for absolute change had miraculously been revived.

Judith said that practicing Artaud demanded immersion in whole-body experiences. In parallel with Artaud's efforts, Beck and the company's plague scene became a sustained attack on spectators' nerves. Over thirty cast members caught in the death throes of a terrible disease would walk through the audience and die right there at their feet. After a few agonizing minutes, other members of the troupe would arrive, two at a time, to take away 'corpses'. As helpers piled up bodies, stiff as kippers, a scene emerged looking unlike anything since the holocaust.

The Living Theatre always roused their audience with this macabre spectacle. In Europe, kids jumped up and 'died' in the aisles on a regular basis just so they could join the body pile; the revolutionary Danny Cohn-Bendit participated in the plague scene of *Mysteries* in France. Other spectators became hostile and agitated. When Judith played dead she created tension: '*In America, it was more common to be treated aggressively. I had been kicked, stomped, tickled, had my fingers bent back, and my hair set on fire.*' [4]

Mysteries inspired Jim Morrison as he sat in the USC auditorium on that Monday night. Morrison had already encountered Artaud as a predecessor. Their similarities were astounding: the two men followed similar roads to freedom. Not for nothing did Jim's UCLA film school contemporary, Bill Kerby, writing in *The Daily Bruin,* call the Doors '*Artaud rock.*' [5]

Jim championed *The Theatre and Its Double.* He also shared an independent interest in Norman O. Brown, another of the Living Theatre's influences. Brown, a Freudian innovator, believed crowds underwent a kind of mass psychosis: a plague. Reviewing The Doors in 1967 (*before* Beck's US tour) *Life* journalist Fred Powledge wrote, '*Everyone with whom I talked about The Doors had made the point their concerts were a lot like The Living Theatre.*' [6]

The plague scene from *Mysteries* stayed with Jim and inspired his next day at work - jamming out surf songs and weird new blues. On what became known as the *Rock is Dead* session, he began toying with Elvis: *Love Me Tender* and *Mystery Train.*[7] *Rock is Dead* implied that corporations had fossilized the last generation's musical impulse making it too decadent, too self-conscious and too dissipated – unable to evoke real hysteria. Jim was ushering in a new era; inviting people to get right down and *die,* at least in a metaphorical sense. He would write about the 'LA plague', expire on stage in *Unknown Soldier*, and preface *The End* by uttering the eerie chant, '*Bring me your dead! Bring me your dead!*' The idea of forgetting, of giving up your old interests and being drawn into a new contagion, was dear to Jim Morrison. It mapped out his road toward freedom.

And the plague, the mystery, the strangeness, kept going that night when Jim returned to USC to watch The Living Theatre's adaptation of *Frankenstein*; an odd, open-text play which evoked an atmosphere of misery and sinister executions to upset the social equilibrium.

Frankenstein ran for two nights, Tuesday and Wednesday, with Beck presiding over escalating terrors as the lanky doctor. The message of the play was simple: can a society born in violence ever survive without it? One actor cawed morosely, '*There was only one means to overcome the sensation of pain - and that was through death!*' [8] In silhouette, somebody's heart got pulled out to supply the monster. Cast-member Jenny Hecht looked up, like some vamp from a silent movie. She would reach out her hands and stare with eyes fixed-open like a seer. Everyone would give a great collective shout and watch the hideous freak slowly tingle with electricity. Made from the entrails of the dead, Frankenstein's creation - a huge acrobatic composite of cast members – railed against its solitude by destroying the set. In an extended finale the actors were then 'arrested' one at a time.

On Thursday night, USC was treated to *Antigone*, Judith Malina's reworking of the ancient Greek tragedy that inspired Bertolt Brecht. She made the play a straight morality tale. *Antigone* had a plot that was both elementary and effective: when civic leaders ignore their citizens' humanity – in this case by punishing Antigone for burying a brother who died in battle - a gruesome comeuppance awaits. Cast members would crawl around in the aisles and Judith always appeared heartbroken in the title role. With tears melting the greasy rim of mascara from her eyes, she resembled a pint-sized Alice Cooper.

Judith's husband Julian liked the play on personal grounds. Both he and Malina were strong characters off stage. They married after he got her pregnant two decades earlier. However, Julian soon realized he was gay and, despite feelings of fondness and loyalty, he could never quite meet her full passion. Over the years Beck remained a distant, flighty figure, and on one occasion he even scarred his wife's forehead with a cigarette. In *Antigone* he got to act the bad guy and it worked out a lot of tension. With apocalyptic reverence, his wife noted that there were earth tremors in West Los Angeles when they started *Antigone* at 9.00pm.

On Friday, The Living Theatre brought its week at USC to a climax with *Paradise Now*. Judith Malina reported there was a lot of hassle about money and locals got uptight about fire laws and exits. A decision was made to seal off the balconies and one policeman rushed up and down between the dressing rooms, swearing he could smell marijuana. Julian sensed trouble and asked for his payment in advance. USC refused. They pointed out that advance payment was not in The Living Theatre's contract so Beck capitulated. After the standoff had kept the audience waiting outside for half an hour - the show went ahead. According to Judith Malina:

> *'The audience, not politicized, got politicized by the situation. They did come up on stage and there wasn't anything the fireman could do that wouldn't have started real trouble. And when the people in the balcony felt the restriction, the children of Paradise lowered a rope and came down into the orchestra, evading guards at the door, and a wild cry of liberation rose up, and everyone felt the example of revolutionary protest was defined.'* [9]

Although The Doors' manager Bill Siddons felt intimidated, Jim loved the show. Sitting in the front row, a lucid, subversive and mischievous Morrison greeted events around him with great enthusiasm.

When everybody stood up, the fire marshal walked out. Then one disgruntled lady beat an intimidating actor with her umbrella. As she got ready to leave, Morrison grabbed her hat and threw it back into the crowd, who applauded his action.

Paradise Now carried on well beyond 11.00pm. It made history at USC as a night of revelry and inspiration - a rock'n'roll moment.

Because they knew the local police were aware of their reputation, the company avoided going nude. Nonetheless the performance was a triumph: '*Forty police cars surrounded the building. The play proceeded in peace. The audience left, exiting between rows of armed-to-the-teeth LA cops with walkie-talkies. Great exhilaration.*' [10]

Finally, after leaving the auditorium, Jim Morrison stumbled back toward Hollywood, charmed.

3
Lamb to the Slaughter

The next morning, March 1st 1969, Jim was supposed to be Miami-bound for the first engagement of a big American tour. His redhead girlfriend Pam Courson came round early and they argued. Magnetism, of course, repels as often as it attracts and the pair could never get it together for very long. They had a fight at the airport and she went home alone. The rest of the band had already boarded for Miami, so Jim was left stranded in the departure lounge. He sought sanctuary where he could always find it, in a bottle. Jack Daniels, Wild Turkey, whatever takes the edge off your tongue.

The Doors allowed themselves twelve hours to travel across the continent. Because Jim didn't show up on time, he missed the 8.00am shuttle to New Orleans. Bill Siddons stayed behind as a chaperone, but was hardly in charge. Once Jim made the first leg of the journey he sat in a New Orleans airport bar for so long that, once again, he missed his eastbound connection.

Finally, at about 8.30pm his car sped into Miami's Coconut

Grove and stopped at the back exit of the Dinner Key auditorium. It was like a scene from hell. Thirteen thousand kids jostled for breathing space in a dimly lit hangar and a further 2,000 tried to force their way inside. The security, a ragged crew of football players and off-duty cops, floated along the footlights like a daisy chain. Most of The Doors - keyboard player Ray Manzarek, drummer John Densmore and guitarist Robby Krieger – had arrived on time, only to find that the local promoters, *Thee Image,* had crammed more kids into the place than everyone agreed; more kids than it could reasonably be expected to hold.

As they waited over an hour for Jim to arrive, the band felt especially anxious. Unlike Amsterdam (where Jim got himself stoned unconscious and Manzarek did the singing) the group could not contemplate playing Miami as a threesome; the local crowd was just too edgy.

Thee Image was a strange crew. Ken Collier and his brother led a team somewhere between a karate club and a concert promotion outfit. They threatened to keep the band's gear hostage in their truck if the musicians didn't play. The Doors had turned down a University of Miami offer to participate in this deal. Now they were being ripped-off by their promoter for over $15,000.[1]

A Doors' rider specified that *Thee Image* should provide two six-packs of beer: after cracking open yet another Corona, Jim was decidedly loose. He'd been drinking for over twelve hours…

The lights went down and Ken Collier introduced his reluctant guests by asking the audience to keep its cool. He walked off stage giving the peace sign. Suddenly a rapt sea of faces caught sight of the band walking on. With two years, three albums and a couple of mighty hit singles behind them, here, live in the flesh, were The Doors!

Because his band missed their usual sound-check, they found it difficult to pull the music together. Yet there was also something else missing. Staggering around in a leather cap with a skull and crossbones on it, Jim hardly lived up to the role of a shaman that night. After begging the front row for additional drinks, Morrison persevered for over an hour and constantly resisting his own musicians. Jim ignored the start of each song, slurred his vocals and sang monotonously. Although he managed to conquer *Back Door Man* he systematically sabotaged *Five To One, Touch Me* and *When The Music's Over.* Just as the crowd started to boil, a peace protester named Louis Marvin approached the stage and handed over a lamb. Jim explained,

> *'He gave it to me in the middle of the show. I just held it for a while. It was really interesting: there was a lot of noise and a lot of commotion - it was almost deafening - in the auditorium, but the lamb was breathing normally, almost purring like a kitten. It was completely relaxed. I guess what they say about "lambs to the slaughter" is true: they don't feel a thing.'* [2]

After handing back the lamb, Morrison continued to fool around. He took his shirt off because somebody poured champagne on it and got everyone moving for the big finale, *Light My Fire.* Ken's brother threatened to stop the show saying, '*Someone's gonna get hurt!*' [3] In response Jim flipped him right off stage. Pandemonium broke out across the whole hangar.

> *'I wanna see you people come on up here and have some fun!'* [4]

They had some fun all right. Someone threw a gallon of bright orange paint over the musicians. The stage began listing off to the left, sinking as teens swarmed all over it. Eventually it broke clean off. Speaker stacks toppled over. Collier pulled the plug.

His wife switched on the house lights and he kicked over Densmore's drums. Next, Larry Pizzi - a karate black-belt - approached Morrison from behind and tripped him into the audience. Wrecked, sodden and minus a shirt, but without a care in the world, Jim led a writhing chain of bodies round the margins of the auditorium. He soon disappeared again and emerged triumphant on the balcony to view the mayhem.

All of it appeared futile in a sense: Morrison the inebriated wild fool taking a stand against the whole planet, again. Since The Doors were poised on the brink of an unprecedentedly large twenty-date tour (Jim had never previously worked for over four gigs in a row) some suggested it was his way to deny the band's capitulation to conformity. Yet he had already done that one way or another. Less than a month earlier he became so unreliable that Densmore and Krieger had walked off stage in Ann Arbor. Densmore was so worried about Jim's unpredictable behaviour, letting down audiences, that he developed a skin-rash. Receiving adulation as the public face of freedom, while feeling trapped at the same time by a lucrative circle of rock'n'roll commitments, Jim attempted to get away from the script. Yet there was more to the Dinner Key evening than the Lizard King's usual antics. After all, inviting the audience on stage was nothing new. He had done that the previous year in Phoenix. Under the surface, the Miami show was at least in part *premeditate*d.

Jim Morrison was nervy and on edge. While his argument with Pam was hardly exceptional, he had made her the sole beneficiary in his will three weeks earlier, it appeared out of step with their recent happiness. Before Miami Jim drank more than usual, but at the concert he also feigned much of his stupor. Morrison was so prepared for his ordeal that he was wearing new boxer shorts. Ray Manzarek said to Robert Matheu of *Creem*, '*I wish he'd have told somebody what he was planning to do.*' [5]

To Manzarek it was clear that Jim had thought ahead about his actions.

Morrison decided to use his inspiration from The Living Theatre because he had been planning to change his public role. Taped for posterity just a few days beforehand, in a kind of elaborate rehearsal for his ordeal, during the *Rock Is Dead* session Jim began saying almost exactly the same comments that he made at the Dinner Key. When the night came he explained to the Miami crowd:

> *'Listen, I used to think that the whole thing was a big joke. I used to think it was something to laugh about. And then the last couple of nights I met some people who were doing something. They're trying to change the world and I want to get on that trip. I wanna change the world... I want to see you people come up and have some fun!'* [6]

He shocked the spectators awake by using The Living Theatre's style of intense verbal repetition as a way to hammer his point home. For nearly an hour Morrison subverted the band, challenged the audience, and offered everyone a glimpse of Paradise Now:

> *'Hey listen, I'm lonely. I need some love, you all... I need you. There's so many of you out there. Nobody's gonna love me, sweet heart, come on...'*
>
> *'How long are you gonna let people push you around? How long? Maybe you like it...'* [7]

As Densmore wondered, '*Why did he want to ruin everything we'd created? ... His charmed life ended in Miami. What was it that drove Jim to the abyss and then made him jump that night, in his home state?*' [8]

Jim was born in Melbourne, a rather non-descript way-station upstate of Miami known mainly for its airport and recreation area. The place is overshadowed by the more popular local attraction Cocoa Beach (grand home of NASA's Kennedy Space Center).

Morrison measured his life-journey geographically, marking out his development by the places he'd been. Two and a half thousand miles from Jim's Florida birthplace, California's west coast was the terminus of Western civilization, a border zone where the night finally met day. He felt his move from the backwaters of Florida to the Wild West of California represented an act of liberation, a throwing-off of authoritarian shackles. On The Doors' first press bio' Morrison explained, *'The world we suggest is a new Wild West. A sensuous, evil world.'* [9]

It was also *his* world. Jim even requested that his ashes be scattered from LA to San Francisco.

He saw his momentary Florida homecoming as an opportunity to confront a constricted past and to stop local youngsters enduring the same oppressions he'd experienced earlier in life.

> *'I ain't talking about revolution... I'm talking about having a good time this summer. Now, you all come out to LA...'* [10]

Afterwards the clean-up operation at the Dinner Key found shirts, blouses and even a few bras all strewn across the floor. The show, for all its silliness, was an oasis of liberation in Florida's uptight environment and those kids had never seen anything like it before.

Although The Living Theatre reached campus radicals and a middle American press hungry for controversy, they remained outside the mainstream: Beck made that decision when he refused to play Broadway. Their work drew its energy from the audience's oppression, but the American excursion had set them against *indifference* from more comfortable adult spectators. However, Jim Morrison – that drunken freedom fighter and eccentric rogue - opened a door between Beck's vision of a new society and the lives of ordinary kids. Through the opening he gave a popular audience a glimpse of Paradise. Making music during a time in-between surf sounds and glam-rock, Morrison emptied a whole series of literary alternatives - Baudelaire, Rimbaud, Nietzsche, Artaud, Burroughs - into pop imagination. He might not have provided The Living Theatre's radical psychosurgery, but he operated on a different level. Jim was an inspiration.

The Dinner Key evening seemed like a joke at the time but it soon gave self-appointed guardians of public culture an excuse to pillory The Doors. Staff writer Larry Mahoney – who had attended Florida State University at the same time as Jim - began hotting things up at the *Miami Herald* office down on the causeway just east of the city centre. On Sunday he co-wrote a piece, 'Disorder Follows Pop Concert.' For his next article, Mahoney threw a moral firecracker across the breakfast tables of the city. Headed 'Rock Group Fails to Stir a Riot,' this one raved:

> 'Morrison, flouting the laws of obscenity, indecent exposure, and incitement to riot, could only stir a minor mob scene... Morrison appeared to masturbate in full view of his audience, screamed obscenities, and exposed himself. He also got violent, slugged several Thee Image officials... At no time was any effort made by the police to arrest Morrison, even when the mob scene on the bandstand got out of hand.' [11]

Mahoney's writing was contradictory: what began as 'Rock Group Fails to Stir a Riot' verbally progressed into a 'minor mob scene' and eventually 'got out of hand.' But despite the discrepancy - his feature created the desired effect. Just when the rock press decided to ignore the story, the *Miami Herald* introduced Jim Morrison to straight readers – Right-thinking middle Americans, adults unfamiliar with the excesses of psychedelic rock. Working from his base at the *Miami Herald*, Mahoney catalysed a firestorm against The Doors with follow-up articles like 'Public Reacts to Rock Show,' 'Disgrace at Dinner Key' and 'Grossed Out by the Doors.' Soon he was left to merely chronicle the events he had set in train: 'Rock Singer Charged,' 'Too Much Restraint Shown in Doors Case,' 'Singer Jim Morrison Guilty of Indecency' and, most ominously, 'Morrison and Miami: Beginning of the End.'

The police department responded with relative indifference at first. Several officers had been drafted in as security for The Doors' concert and, in 1969, $4.50 an hour was nice overtime if you could get it. Of course there was a bit of shoving around outside the Dinner Key beforehand, and the kids laughed when Jim stole a policeman's hat, but no one got seriously hurt. Life went on. Nobody seemed especially changed. Nevertheless Larry Mahoney began making phone calls.

Although the Dinner Key was located in the bohemian Coconut Grove district, it was a public auditorium located just a parking-lot away from City Hall. To keep the story cooking after the first article, Mahoney asked civic leaders what they intended to do about the cause of outrage and, by Tuesday, the circuit court judge Arthur Huttow (president of the Crime Commission of Greater Miami) called for a full-scale investigation. He smelled a conspiracy - maybe even a police cover-up.

Almost overnight the weight of the *Miami Herald's* readership was brought to bear on an apparently sloppy local police force. Acting Chief Paul Denham immediately responded to Mahoney's biting observation that 'at no time was any effort made by the police to arrest Morrison.' [12] Denham told the *Herald's* readers that he had every intention to follow it up and had issued orders to take out a warrant for the singer's arrest as soon as he could find a policeman who witnessed the incident.

As keen readers of the *Miami Herald*, the local FBI was on Jim Morrison's case like a bullet. On Tuesday March 4th Kenneth Whittaker, the Bureau's head man in Miami, sent a major report as part of COINTELPRO, the counter-intelligence program. The report was so significant that Whittaker, in his role as 'Special Agent in Charge', dispatched eleven copies to the FBI's Washington head office.

Marked 'Possible Racial Violence - Major Urban Areas - Racial Matters,' the memo dealt mostly with civil rights in Greater Miami. In the wake of Martin Luther King's death the previous year, King's co-worker Ralph Abernathy held a press conference to challenge Republicans from inside their Miami Beach convention.

Following Abernathy's forthright yet ponderous speech, more than sixty members of the Poor People's Campaign demonstrated black unity by raising Soul Power salutes in the lobby of the convention building. Six miles across the city a riot broke out that night. Three people were killed and five critically injured as Miami policemen exchanged gunfire with snipers. National Guardsmen had to recapture the city block by block and local authorities made over one hundred and fifty arrests. Nixon was really shaken by the interruption. Nobody wanted to be caught unaware by a repeat performance, so the FBI scrambled agents to monitor the black community. Miami's 'first black-operated shopping center' was about to open and Whittaker was so on edge that he checked one hundred and ten local sources for signs of trouble.

The Bureau constantly reinterpreted COINTELPRO to legitimise its pursuit of new subversives, irrespective of evidence about their potential for danger. Tacked on the end of Whittaker's report was a briefing about a 'rock and roll singer' named Jim Morrison. According to the information obtained, Morrison:

> ...reportedly pulled out all the stops in an effort to provoke chaos among a huge crowd of young people. Morrison's program lasted one hour during which time he sang one song and for the remainder he grunted, groaned, gyrated and gestured along with inflammatory remarks. He screamed obscenities and exposed himself which resulted in a number of people on stage being hit and slugged and thrown to the floor.

The identity of Kenneth Whittaker's 'source' is not hard to uncover: Larry Mahoney's account from the previous day's *Miami Herald* had been duplicated in the COINTELPRO report. His sensational description now existed on a different level, as a reason for official government business. He'd mentioned that thirty-one off-duty cops had been hired to organize security by the Dinner Key promoters. A local investigation was being conducted. Morrison would definitely be charged with misdemeanours.

Under typical police practice, warrants are usually sworn in for *already-indicted* criminals who fail to attend court. To issue a warrant for somebody who is not yet charged - and is not, therefore, currently recognized as a criminal - is rare indeed. It is reserved for offenders who commit especially serious crimes.

Misdemeanours aren't enough. So Whittaker continued:

> In addition, the matter will be discussed with the Florida State Attorney's Office to determine if Morrison can be charged with a felony.[13]

In other words, the FBI was making sure that this loud, crude 'rock and roll singer' would find himself swimming in very deep water. Nailing Morrison with a felony would prevent him walking away, salvage Dade County's public reputation and, if necessary, allow the Bureau to get involved in Jim's extradition case. It was a masterstroke of politics by means of law enforcement.

The Assistant State Attorney Alfonso Sepe was running for judgeship. When informed about this situation he saw an opportunity to make his name. Together with another opportunist prosecutor and their assistant Terence McWilliams, Sepe took steps to compile the case. Once he had obtained a hundred and fifty photos of the evening, all he needed was a witness willing to sign a complaint. The events at Dinner Key could then be categorized as a felony.

Asking around at the prosecutor's office, Sepe found two interns who had a relative working as a clerk on the sixth floor of the Justice Building. The clerk, Bob Jennings, had attended The Doors' show and was willing to sign a complaint. Jennings' complaint in turn authorized Chief Denham to take investigative action. An internal police department inquiry was launched to question the off-duty staff employed as security at the Dinner Key, as well as a few kids who volunteered information. Sepe and Denham stuck to three particular crimes: lewd and lascivious behaviour, public intoxication, and indecent exposure. On

Wednesday March 5th the City of Miami issued six warrants for Morrison's arrest.[14]

Ambiguities certainly existed, not least a distinct vagueness about what people had expected from the singer: teeny-bop sex symbol or scathing rebel? Many of the band's recordings sounded deep and sinister: not exactly bobby-sox fare. It was, in fact, the University of Miami's student crowd - liberal young adults – who had first asked The Doors to come to Florida. At least one key question also lingered around the memory of Jim's actions: had he actually exposed himself? The *Miami Herald* seemed to clear up any doubts. According to them Jim Morrison - perpetually touted as '*the self-styled "King of Orgasmic Rock"*' - gave an '*obscene performance before 10,000 teenagers...*' [15]

The same day that Mahoney's first article lambasted The Doors, on the opposite coast of America USC cancelled The Living Theatre's two remaining shows under the pretext of a fire regulation. Luckily an alternative community had offered the troupe free accommodation in San Francisco. They drove up the west coast immediately.

Above the famous City Lights bookstore down on the Haight, six of the actors made Lawrence Felinghetti's office The Living Theatre's temporary headquarters. Their sleeping bags lay alongside shelves full of modern literature. Heading north was a good idea as the company gradually felt their troubles ebb away. After a few hours of phone calls, the Inland Revenue Service suddenly stopped badgering promoter Saul Gottlieb over Julian's tax arrears. His players were also managing to break even with well-received performances at the Straight Theatre.

When Jim Morrison found that the troupe had moved on, he went to San Francisco, accompanied by the McClures, looking for inspiration. On Saturday March 8th Jim watched an exhausted company on their third performance of the day, doing *Paradise Now* at the Straight Theatre and according to Judith Malina he participated with enthusiasm. Morrison and Michael McClure did a great number on race relations in the Capetown scene. The next day they strolled down the Haight.

When a younger Jim Morrison lived in Almeda, on weekends he would take the bus to San Francisco and creep round the City Lights bookstore, too anxious to approach Lawrence Ferlinghetti. Yet the weekend after everything went mad in Miami, new friends invited him inside Ferlinghetti's private office. At last he had an opportunity to talk to the leaders of The Living Theatre. Judith Malina noted:

> '*All day there are financial problems - Equity, the boat tickets, the New York Office - and long negotiations that come to nothing but: there's no money for our boat tickets. In the midst of this crisis Mike McClure and Joanna McClure come to visit us and we sit around and talk lazily. They have bought Jim Morrison (of the Doors), who is very quiet and easygoing. We eat honey... Julian talks on the phone about the desperate money matters, and Morrison, who says very little, offers to help.*
>
> *He'll send money.*' [16]

They discussed students, Paradise, politics and literature. After three more days Judith reported, '*Jim Morrison gives us twenty-five hundred dollars. Saves our skins.*' [17]

By giving The Living Theatre that life-saving donation, Morrison stood shoulder to shoulder with an army of people pressing for change in society; a group he greatly admired. At a time when factions were divided and revolution seemed near, he joined the wealth of patrons contributing to The Living Theatre. Jim's donation aligned him with Ferlinghetti and the beatniks; with

William Carlos Williams, Tennessee Williams and Martin Buber; with the May '68 revolutionary Daniel Cohn-Bendit, and with the other luminaries who supported Julian Beck's productions.

After Jim offered the money, both parties – Judith and the McClures, Jim and Julian – resumed their discussions about life, art and freedom. Like Julian, Jim was *not* interested in a bloody revolution or re-inhabiting existing structures. He sought a more subtle and more lasting prize: *a revolution of the soul.*

The conversation was positive but short-lived. Less than three weeks after their Californian visit, The Living Theatre was gone.

Meanwhile a storm of outrage was brewing in Miami. Early in March, it didn't feel so serious to The Doors. They shrugged off the over-reaction and even found it laughable. The group had a Caribbean vacation lined up. In Jim's absence, with lightning speed the newspapers turned his behaviour into a matter of public interest. They had catalysed a civil procedure, then seized the drama that they had created, and milked it for all it was worth. Morrison was in real trouble. A circle of words began to gather like a noose round the singer's neck. Soon he faced the threat of a humiliating spell in jail. He was being demonized down in Florida.

None of America's sixties radicals found incarceration a pleasant prospect, but some treated their temporary stops behind bars as a necessary evil. To The Living Theatre, jail was simply an occupational hazard on the road to non-violent revolution. The prison-house of civilization had *already* locked its doors around the human heart, confining its inhabitants within a cast iron legacy of their own ideas. Having explored social opposition through theatre for the last three decades, Julian Beck and Judith Malina had already accumulated an arrest record as long as your arm. Their harassment by the police rapidly became nothing but a drag. As Beck told Aldo Rostagno:

> *'A good guerrilla theatre has to have a certain flexibility that we - maybe because of the 'old age' coming upon us - don't have. The performers should be able to afford to get busted every other time they play. The Living Theatre really can't, because we won't be able to go into a new city, sooner or later. We can't afford to go out in the streets at the end of Paradise Now and get arrested every time. We couldn't afford to play in Brooklyn without promising the police chief that we were not going to do this. Our heaviness, our being a big establishment, our having forty people to support and nine babies, our having a history - all these things are terrible limitations.'* [18]

On the other hand, rather than frustration, Jim greeted the possibility of confinement with great fear. According to The Doors' equipment manager Vince Treanor, '*He was terrified of jail.*'[19] How could a roving libertine like Morrison - a man who veritably *lived* for the cause of freedom - face life inside Raiford, Florida's elite penal institution? More than anything it would contradict his 'no limits - no laws' philosophy.

Of course nobody is as simple as one wooden idea, but Jim's whole public persona was based on his voyage: internal freedom through external revolt. He was *untamed.* Prison would not only break him personally. To the public who followed The Doors it would contradict his whole philosophy and crush everything he represented.

Down in the humid recesses of his own State, where cops with crew-cuts chewed gum and stared without mercy, Jim faced the ironic prospect of being felled by a parody of his own image.

4

Some Way To Stop It

Larry Mahoney's shock waves of print made Jim Morrison's life a misery. Slowly but surely they reverberated across several different fields, one of which was the live music scene. The Concert Hall Managers Association criticized The Doors in their newsletter and recommended that each venue make the promoter post an advanced security bond of $5,000 per gig, in case of a costly arrest or cancellation. Meanwhile The Doors' booking agency Ashley Famous came up with an excuse for Jim's behaviour: he was only tucking in his pants!

As word spread through the industry, the bookers for The Doors' upcoming tour cancelled every date one by one. A state legislator wrote to Jacksonville's mayor urging him to stop the group's next engagement. From there to Salt Lake City, almost overnight, $18,000 in advanced ticket sales went down the drain. All sixteen States cancelled. The biggest live act in America was unemployable and the stigma that was created in Miami refused to go away.

Chapter 4

As soon as the band began to appear again, local promoters and police took all sorts of harsh precautions. When The Doors played Mexico City, five months after Miami, top hotels refused to take them. *El Heraldo* called the band 'hippies' and 'undesirables.' Their label Elektra even postponed an attempt to record them for the *Absolutely Live* album at the Whiskey in May. Instead the label did it three months later when the band played LA's Aquarius Theater. What began as a joke eventually cost The Doors over $100,000 dollars in lost revenue and countless hours in court. It left Jim Morrison's future unresolved. The events of that wild evening in Miami followed him around like a curse.

The fire was gone from The Doors' live show. When the group played live together their spiritual feelings had already begun to disappear. Now there was no chance of recapturing the shaman's dynamite on stage. Jim's band-mates, especially John, felt they had also taken the blame for his immorality. It was one thing to put up with a little silliness and irresponsibility; this seemed more like involuntary collective suicide.

From Jim's point of view, the other three members' conventional attitude to making money in the Mu$ic Business could only cause friction. By staying true to his original ethics, he felt wrenched by the contradictions that his band-mates had ignored. Still expressing rebellion - while being reminded that an entourage depended on him - he saw himself drawn into more and more hypocrisy. What started out as a communal mission to change the world was just becoming another regular job. Bill Siddons said that the Dinner Key's aftermath nearly caused the end of The Doors.

Even *fans* took Miami as a kind of personal betrayal. Suddenly everybody had heard about Jim Morrison and, even though concerned parents knew very little about the man, they didn't like the sound of him. The fuss over Morrison was even making his fans look bad. Furthermore, his behaviour had cost them the opportunity to see him live in concert.

Jim could barely understand it. He told his New York friend Patricia Kennealy, '*It's like they thought I'd betrayed them. But they were the ones who seemed to want it. No matter what I did it was never enough; they always wanted something weirder or grosser or wilder.*' [1] They pushed him to the limit and now he'd gone over the edge: '*I think I was just fed up with the image that had been created around me.*' [2]

Miami turned out to be a giant misunderstanding. Morrison wanted to change the world - his own world, and that of others. But by rejecting one particular image he had facilitated something worse.

On Northwest Eighth Avenue in central Miami, not far from the city port, stands the Orange Bowl: an imposing Pro Player stadium that hosts the King Orange Jamboree Parade and annual football game. Just four days after Chief Denham issued Jim's initial warrant, Jean Wardlow of the *Miami Herald* chronicled a new plan: 'Clean Teens Rally for Scour Power.' In response to the Dinner Key evening, this 'Rally for Decency' was held inside the Orange Bowl on March 23rd. Hosted by the comedian Jackie Gleason, it featured the actresses Kate Smith and Anita Bryant, as well as Miami's Drum & Bugle Corps.

The Decency movement was a bigger publicity stunt than The Doors' Dinner Key show could ever have been. A crowd of 30,000 teens and adults, more than twice the number at the Dinner Key gathering, showed that Miami detested their recent visitors from LA. Rally organizer Mike Levesque, a seventeen-year-old high school student, realized that a crusade for Decency might take him places. He told the newspapers that the TV show *Today* had promised him a guest slot. Invitations to organize rallies elsewhere arrived from four other cities. Levesque became a public celebrity, a moral entrepreneur.

At that time Richard Nixon held America's highest office. Jim had already stated his opinion of the Republican president: playing a gig after Nixon's election in 1968 he said, '*Four more years of mediocrity... If he does wrong, we will get him.'*[3] Now, it appeared, the boot was squarely on the other foot. Three days after the Orange Bowl event, Mike Levesque received a letter of support from the White House.

President Nixon had good reason to help Miami. In August of the previous year the Miami Beach area had been transformed into Nixonville. At the Republican convention that suffered Abernathy's poverty protest, the middlebrow senator beat Nelson Rockefeller and Ronald Reagan to win the Republican Party's presidential candidacy. Since then, he had conquered the national election and been installed in the Oval Office.

The new president led with a decidedly bureaucratic style. Norman Mailer reported,

> *'It was as if Richard Nixon were proving that a man who had never spent an instant inquiring whether family, state, church, and flag were ever wrong could go in secure steps, denuded of risk, from office to office until he was president.'* [4]

Certainly Nixon tried his best to avoid rocking the boat. Instead he aimed to keep everybody on board, even as it drifted into deeper and deeper water. In his nomination speech, he told the assembled press that he pledged to bring an end to the war in Vietnam. Six months later, of course, the war continued.

The whole logic of the Decency movement - 'I am entirely decent, you are indecent, and I say where the line is drawn' - lent itself to laundering the reputations of the mighty. Each rally offered the great and the good a plum opportunity to whitewash their names.[5] Jim Morrison, a drunken twenty-five year old - who *might* have publicly exposed himself for eight seconds - became the epitome of the class 'indecent'. Richard Nixon, the man who sent tens of thousands of young people to face savage, unnecessary deaths in some foreign jungle, could *appear* 'decent' just because he made it known that he supported the Clean Teens movement.

Just over three weeks after the Dinner Key show a letter marked 'Personal and Highly Confidential' found its way to FBI headquarters in Washington. Addressed to the 'Honorable J. Edgar Hoover, Director', it read:

> I thought you would be interested in the enclosed record disc and my letter to Senator Sam J. Ervin, Jr. As mentioned to Senator Ervin, I don't know what, if anything, can be done to stop the dissemination of such trash, but I believe we must find some way to stop it.
>
> The thought occurred to me that you might want to discuss this with the Attorney General and that - hopefully - the two of you might be able to do something. Certainly, the great majority of decent Americans will applaud any efforts to make record racks and newsstands refrain from peddling such filth.

Enclosed with the message were copies of the letter to Senator Ervin, a clipping about Jim in Miami, and a record by The Fugs called *Virgin Fugs (For Adult Minds Only)*. The whole package came from Charles H. Crutchfield.

Crutchfield was an ex-agent - an old friend of the Bureau who remained on its Special Correspondents List. Like most men choosing the generous option of early retirement, he had taken up a second career. Charles Crutchfield became the president of

Jefferson Standard Broadcasting, a chain of radio stations he ran from Charlotte in North Carolina. He wanted to clean up America and today he was pulling no punches.

His other correspondent, Sam Ervin - a folksy, bible-quoting man soon to become famous for his role presiding over Watergate – was Charles Crutchfield's local representative. Crutchfield asked Ervin (himself a friend of the Bureau, who praised them in 1971) to discuss the matter with Senator Everett Dirksen, the highest-ranking Republican in congress. It was a smart move. In effect, well over a decade before the PMRC tried to censor popular music, Charles Crutchfield went straight to the top of America's political and judicial systems and attempted to stop rock'n'roll's animal excess. He appealed to the FBI director's image-consciousness and threw in some knee-jerk patriotism.

Hoover shifted uncomfortably in his chair. Despite being seventy-four years old, the director remained firm and unshakable. He never gave up, never retired. J. Edgar Hoover simply followed one line of thinking. For him renegade rockers were not just a legal matter but represented a much deeper problem, something from way back before any of The Fugs or Jim Morrison was born…

John Edgar Hoover was appointed director of the Bureau in 1924. Paranoid about his unit's precious public reputation, in the 1930s Hoover thought that America faced a bigger problem than crime: a fugitive popular culture. The wily flair of gangsters inspired each new generation as it fell in love with trashy movies and high-circulation pulps. Hoodlums and thieves like Bonnie and Clyde, Pretty Boy Floyd and John Dillinger were national heroes. Evil aroused more fascination than Good. How could a law enforcement agency operate efficiently when the general public rooted for the criminals?

In a campaign to win back the nation, Hoover responded by employing the talents of pulp-scribe Courtney Ryley Cooper and former *Brooklyn Eagle* correspondent Henry Suydam. They engineered a new image: the white, male, all-American law-enforcer - the G-man - whose swift crime-fighting skills and high-handed morality could always be counted on to save the day. With Cooper and Suydam writing the script, the baddies ended up where they belonged: behind bars.

To rejuvenate the white knight image, Hoover constantly looked for new enemies of the Bureau. In days past he had demonized anarchists, gangsters and communists. By the 1960s he found his foes *within* America. Blacks, pacifists, terrorists and unpatriotic students kept breaking out like boils on the face of a good country. By offering money and generous draft deferments, FBI representatives secretly recruited students as informants and infiltrated college campuses. The Bureau's invisible network mobilized suspicion against liberal teachers and systematically dismantled the freedom of ideas. America teetered on the brink between fascism and freedom. And in the midst of all this came rock musicians: new enemies who were, as an example of personal liberation, writ large for the youth of the nation.

A week after The Fugs album arrived, Hoover passed it on to Robert Mahoney of the Bureau's General Investigative Division for a decision on prosecution.[6] The Fugs were an off-off Broadway band: the brainchild of Ed Sanders, Ken Weaver and Tuli Kupferberg. Together they played songs with lyrics based on an unlikely combination of high poetry, expletives and locker-room humour. Judith Malina called Sanders '*the most sophisticated of the poets*' and Julian remembered a New York peace protest where The Fugs' leader burned his draft card.[7] A Bureau memo explained:

> This group is described as New York's most fantastic protest rock and roll peace-sex-grass psychedelic singing group, who write all their own material utilizing the artistic and literary heritage of the lower East Side of New York combined with [inspiration from the] civil rights and peace movements.

Agents in New York had discovered that The Fugs had helped to start the Youth International Party - the infamous 'Yippies'. The Assistant US Attorney Stephen Kaufman deemed The Fugs' first album '*not… a good vehicle for prosecution under the Interstate Transportation of Obscene Matters Statute.*'

The Fugs were only an *underground* band: *small timers.* Putting them on trial would have been counterproductive. It might have given them the oxygen of publicity. Almost twenty years later Tuli Kupferberg recalled, '*Well, we were never arrested, which is amazing. We were threatened many times. Ed had these FBI adversaries... There were suggestions that we'd be prosecuted but nothing ever happened.*' [8]

The Doors were bigger game. But could Crutchfield's complaint strategy really work? It required the cooperation of Hoover, the Attorney General, and Everett Dirksen.

Senator Dirksen made congratulatory public speeches to agents graduating from the Bureau's academy in Quantico, yet behind the scenes Hoover never trusted him. By poking around in Dirksen's particular closet of shady financial dealings, the FBI accumulated its own invaluable, scandal-ready file on the man - the kind of file that worked just because its subject knew you had it. Maybe for that reason, in a senate speech about the 'Rometsch affair' two years later, chairman Dirksen (of the Subcommittee on Constitutional Rights) vetoed a probe into the Bureau's abuse of its mandate.

Also J. Edgar Hoover's relationship with his *official* boss - the Attorney General - was rather unstable. For over forty years, Hoover had used his army of field agents (who now numbered over 7,000 across the country) to prepare for potential showdowns by accumulating whatever dirt they could find on people in high places. Consequently, although each blackmailed Attorney General was in Hoover's pocket, the FBI's director still felt frustrated that he had never acquired his boss's job. In truth it would not have made much difference. Hoover was already able to, literally, call the shots.

All this meant that the kind of high level co-operation Crutchfield requested would not have been easy to achieve. His censorship-by-majority idea would have probably been neglected, even if nothing else stood in its way. However, there was an even more pressing problem. Although Crutchfield asked the Bureau to attack organs of news for peddling filth (things like *Rolling Stone* and, ironically, the *Miami Herald*), the FBI could hardly have challenged the constitutional freedom of the press.

Hoover was hamstrung on that one. A couple of days later he cordially replied:

> I, too, share your concern regarding this type of recording, which is being distributed throughout the country, and certainly appreciate your bringing it to my attention. It is repulsive to right-thinking people and can have serious effects on our young people.

Short of changing American's Freedom of Speech amendment, the FBI's long-running director could do very little to censor the voices of late '60s rock. But J. Edgar Hoover was a very cunning and relentless man. Sitting tight in his Washington office, he knew many ways to bring down his enemies.

Hoover got married to America, but he could never quite control her. Jim Morrison was the illegitimate descendant of their marriage.

Look at the similarities. Both Hoover and Morrison were Southerners, loners, and draft dodgers. Both became famous performers and writers in different ways. They were both manipulators with attention-seeking tendencies. Both surrounded themselves with a small retinue of followers: men they paid not to tell them the truth. And both saw defending the freedom of their country as part of their mandate.

Spot the lineage: Jim's father Steve came from a generation of Hooverite Republicans who grew up admiring G-men as authoritarian tough guys. In charge of the *Bon Homme Richard* - 'The Bonny Dick' – Steve Morrison became the youngest admiral in the entire US navy. While his son attended university, he sailed his great aircraft carrier into the Gulf of Tonkin, increasing the threat of a war in Vietnam.

By the end of the 1960s Steve Morrison's work took him to the Pentagon. In the grand social scheme of things his son might have become a military man or diplomat. Jim's 1961 George Washington high school photograph shows a seventeen year old with a suit, tie and short hair; the young Morrison resembled a moody G-man.

Somewhere along the line Jim escaped his fate. Hoover accepted agents aged twenty-five or above. A twenty-five year old Jim Morrison asked the youth of Miami, '*How long are you going to let people push you around? How long?? Maybe you like it?*' [9] Hoover expelled alcoholics from the FBI. Jim Morrison was one. Hoover hated intellectuals. Morrison went to university. Hoover lived with his mother. Jim Morrison disowned his parents. Hoover refused change. Jim Morrison said he wanted to change the world. Hoover thrived on repression, Morrison on liberation.

What happened? What made Jim deviate from the conventional future that forebears held out for him?

Hoover became highly sophisticated using the power of an institution against its interns. Half a century his junior, Jim Morrison didn't like institutions. He avoided his family, got kicked out of the boy scouts for swearing, never attended graduation and made erratic progress with his band. But - apart from contemplating marriage - he stayed in touch with one particular institution, one sense of belonging: America.

You can blame it on the beats. Reacting to the suffocating hypocrisy of the 1950s, the beatnik movement was a cultural meditation on what America could become. They prayed that, between westward migration and personal change, their native land would be liberated one generation at a time.

During the beatnik era the UCLA students slowly began building Kerouac's hip, wild, free country from LA *inwards*, mounting a takeover from the margin of their own continent. In his controversial sociology of beat lifestyles *The Holy Barbarians*, Lawrence Lipton observed:

> '*It is Sunday in Venice... To this area of Los Angeles, as to similar areas of large cities, have come the rebellious, the nonconformist, the bohemian, the deviant among youth... If you're a UCLA student shacking up with your girlfriend, for love or just to save on some rent, you can find here a ramshackle three- or four-room cottage...*' [10]

Jim Morrison arrived in Venice about five years too late, but decided to recreate the beat ideals of his own accord. In this sense Morrison was never un-American. The Orange Bowl organizers thought they had exclusive rights to America: they handed out 10,000 small flags and opened the event with a public pledge of allegiance. But their rite was a re-purification; Jim Morrison had already emerged as the latest mutation in the bloodline of his country. While other psychedelic groups sometimes burned the US flag, The Doors occasionally performed in front of it. Citizen Jim remained committed to the end. He even wanted to be back from his fated Paris stopover by the 4th of July.

Morrison once told the *Rolling Stone* writer Jerry Hopkins that wanting to be president is a logical extension of being American. Ray Manzarek thought his friend would be an ideal candidate for the White House in later years, but President Morrison would inevitably have entered on an unusual ticket: taking the country on a post-beat joyride. Helping individuals free themselves from those dark structures - materialism, corporate loyalty, fear for the future - which strangle creativity and independence.

Perhaps it is fairest to say that, despite their diametric opposition, Jim and Edgar both responded to the same promise. Both reacted to each other. Each aimed to pull America into a different future. Hoover thought he could safeguard his country's purity by holding back signs of change. But, as Morrison knew, purity was a dangerous idea.[11]

With his interest in ancient mysticism, Jim Morrison aimed to forget by remembering old ways. Ditch the suit, awaken the mind and demand the world, NOW. By accepting both sides of his personality, Morrison embodied America's *inherent impurity*. He straddled the differences in order to set himself up as a healer. The Establishment saw no need to be 'healed'. Instead they decided to erase him.

It didn't seem to matter that Jim's group The Doors differed from the majority of hippies. Not only did the *Miami Herald* make him notorious with parents as a personification of debauchery and symbol of everything bad about the counterculture; the singer also became a target for people like Levesque and Crutchfield, points-scoring entrepreneurs. As Jim explained it, '*The audience that was there* [at the Dinner Key] *really enjoyed it. I think people reading about it in the paper - this distorted version - created a climate of hysteria.*' [12]

The FBI's director loved hysteria. He could use the mesmeric grip it had on people to gain their assent for his cunning plans. Hoover began to see a chance to promote the Bureau. Whittaker's report alerted the director to the name 'Jim Morrison'.[13] Crutchfield's war on 'filth' showed him that disgust was spreading right across America. Even President Nixon was in on this opportunity. As more and more evidence about the scale of disapproval landed on J. Edgar Hoover's desk, he began to recognize a sterling opportunity. Something had to be done.

The Dinner Key controversy may also have struck a chord with the Bureau's leader because he considered Miami every inch his home turf. For the last thirty years Edgar and his blond buddy Clyde Tolson had taken their Christmas vacation down in South Florida. He would subject the local FBI chief Kenneth Whittaker to long chats in the back of his $10,000 limousine. Whittaker said later that Hoover's death in 1972 felt like losing a father.[14] Without fail, the director would take a journey to the Hialeah racetrack and indulge in some good old-fashioned gambling. It was such a fun game that he eliminated all distractions. On Saturdays even the president could not reach him.

Furthermore, the FBI's Miami field office had good connections with the local police. Nationally, FBI agents only constitute one percent of law enforcement officers, yet they seem to get most of the credit. In 1969 they were better paid, better qualified and held in higher esteem than the cops. Local forces had to turn a blind eye when they bumped into agents sneaking around and planting bugs in various places. The Feds also reclaimed cases completed by the cops for the purpose of their own FBI statistics drives. Disputes and mix-ups became commonplace because the police never felt accountable to Hoover and his boys. Ordinarily this caused resentment. Tensions existed between the ranks. But Miami was no ordinary precinct. Federal agents and the Miami police felt a bond of community spirit because Earl Wilson Purdy, an ex-agent, ran the local police precinct. On March 26th, the same day as his reply to Charles Crutchfield, Hoover set the wheels in motion.[15]

5
The Fugitive

A phone rang in the Dade County Justice Building. Yes, Morrison had been charged. No, he wasn't around. His whereabouts was unknown. Police hadn't arrested him on the spot, they said, for fear of provoking the crowd. They wanted to avoid a spontaneous riot. In fact, despite Whittaker's report (that Morrison made an 'effort to provoke chaos') nobody pressed charges for incitement to riot. As Jim would say later, '*We never really had any riots. I mean, a riot is more an out of control and real violent thing. We never had too much of what I would call a real riot.*'[1]

Judicially, Morrison's case remained a local matter. But with publicity growing around the incident and pressure from above, on March 27th US Commissioner Edward P. Swan issued a new warrant which classified 'James Douglas Morrison' - the name Jim kept for his poetry – as a fugitive from justice.

The next day Kenneth Whittaker notified Hoover and the FBI's Special Investigative Division via an internal memorandum. Miami circulated Morrison's full description and warrants to

Tampa, Jacksonville, New York and San Diego. The National Crime Information Centre in Washington also publicized Jim's details. Even though the singer had yet to find it out, police could detain him at will. Miami's Chief Denham proudly told the gathered press, '*We'll extradite him to Miami from any place on earth.*'[2]

Ironically, the idea of Jim as fugitive has a certain ring to it. The Doors formed a *band*: illegitimate leaders, aiming for world domination freewheeling across America with a price on their heads. Unlike other bands they appeared decidedly *secretive*. In one of Hoover's books, the spy Harry Gold confessed that he was bored with '*waiting on street corners in strange towns where I had no business to be and killing time in cheap movies.*'[3] It was as if he knew the slow agony of being a musician on tour. In fact The Doors were all fugitives in their own way. They represented a dare that got out of control, a last flare against authority. Emerging rootless and footloose from LA's lost margin, they roamed America like some bawdy band of minstrels. And despite their talents, they began as young drifters who might otherwise have slipped into obscurity. Densmore looked half-anonymous and Krieger wore dark glasses most of the time. You never knew quite where they had come from - or when they'd be back. In a book on organized subversion, J. Edgar Hoover described the shadowy world of the fugitive:

> To understand the underground we must realize that it is a maze of undercover couriers, escape routes, hide-outs, and clandestine meetings... Sometimes departures have been so rapid that hot meals have been left on the table.[4]

In Doors publicity shots, the group looked as if they'd been disturbed from a secret conversation. Ray Manckzerak - the keyboard player with an East European heritage and subversive intellect – had changed his name. Meanwhile James became Jimbo: the ringleader. He posed for pictures with such a surly look that he resembled a Californian pimp. He seemed about to throw you out of his apartment. Or perhaps he was busted, his face an awkward mixture of resentment and regret.

That image was calculated. Morrison prioritized archetypal characters as a way to realise his art. He loved to impersonate Marlon Brando's lead from *The Fugitive Kind.* According to Hoover:

> Once underground, the member is made ready for assignment. This means, first of all, assuming a new identity; that is, being made into 'another person.' As a general rule this involves the securing of a new name, date, and place of birth, and even changing physical appearance... he would need a 'new identity,' or, in espionage language, a 'change of feathers.'[5]

Among Jim Morrison's preferred 'changes of feathers' (the poet, the sailor, the preacher...) the *hitchhiker* became a recurring persona. Before he was famous he had hitched around the South with his friend Bryan Gates, going right down to Cuidad Juarez in Mexico. Later on, in his film *HWY*, Jim played the Kid - a mysterious figure asking for a lift in the desert.

The hitchhiker: cold and lonely, out on the highway. Hungry. Afraid of wolves and even of his own shadow. He was compelled to leave in order to escape confining relationships - the inner binds of home – but nowadays he never quite felt like he belonged. He always moved as a stranger amongst strangers.

And as a free creature Morrison connected with that symbol of modern life, the stray cat. A sly black cat echoes across The

Doors' sound. You can hear it in the wailing guitar of *People Are Strange* and *Cars Hiss By My Window.* The cat is always unaccountable. It goes where it pleases. Seedy bars and cheap motel rooms. Morrison was a stray.

Only after Jim Morrison escaped his own beginning could he find his destiny. As a hitchhiker, he personified the outsider-come-within: helped but not in debt; invited but never loyal; an escaper and a seeker, focused and purposeful. Dangerously unknown. The hitchhiker's disturbing aura leaves him open to abuse from others who use him as a vehicle for their own change. But he can also dig his claws in as the agent of another's fate, a walking comeuppance. Maybe a fugitive or even a killer.

Wandering, meandering, drifting. Jim Morrison hitched a ride on his family, his band, his record label, his publishers, the press, and even on his own friends. In the early days he began some gigs standing in the audience, heckling his own band. Then he would mount the stage - the changeling. The truth was that, although fugitive status played right in to Jim's misbegotten, rawhide image, perhaps he was looking for something that had already found him.

The FBI made Jim's predicament a reality with *real* consequences: not just some press-call to be tossed off for the sake of entertainment. They operated with a deadly seriousness of purpose. And for them, the fugitive warrant represented a masterstroke.

FBI agents first deployed the label 'fugitive' during the 1930s depression. For most of his career Hoover ignored the racketeers, white-collar fraudsters and all the rest, going instead for high profile villains - bank robbers, kidnappers and 'top hoodlums'. A criminal's publicity value could be completely out of proportion with their wrongdoing, but in the public relations strategy of the FBI, fugitive status became Hoover's trump card. It made the Bureau look good by making the bad guys look nasty.

The issuing of a fugitive warrant moved Morrison's case within the legal remit of the Bureau. It added an extra crime, 'unlawful flight to avoid prosecution'. Fugitive status raised the penalties around Jim, and gave his investigation a higher profile.

In the same year that they handled Jim Morrison's case, the FBI pursued almost 19,000 fugitives. The public already knew Jim so his case was different. He was a prominent singer and, after Miami, a notorious one too. Even though in reality the Bureau had much more pressing things to investigate - like the 40,000 protest bombings that took place in 1969, with Jim it could be *seen* to be doing its job. Instead of following up vital (but low profile) cases, agents devoted their time to bracketing a drunken rock star with murderers, drug lords and others who represented the nation's top criminals…

Two days after Swan signed the warrant, Jim found out that they'd classified him a fugitive. Nobody could quite believe it. He immediately put through a call to the LA lawyer, Max Fink, a dumpy, amiable man in his early sixties who was a Beverly Hills attorney of considerable experience. The band enlisted him at the start of their career after Robby Krieger's father recommended the man. Although he was accustomed to pulling Jim from awkward scrapes, none had ever been quite so big - big enough that when Jim heard the news he *immediately* contradicted his defiant reputation and went straight to the authorities.

On April 3rd the two men made their way to the FBI field office on Wilshire Boulevard. As he sheepishly walked into the busy reception area, Jim probably felt like Max's prodigal son. He might have noticed the unimpeachable face of J. Edgar Hoover staring down from a Dorian Grey type portrait – all field offices displayed a copy.

The rock'n'roll 'fugitive' appeared before a US Commissioner who set a hearing for almost exactly one year's time. Bailed on a corporate surety bond of $5,000, he left promptly. Fink said there was no point in waiving Jim's extradition. A memo sent from LA to the FBI headquarters in Washington explained that Jim Morrison of The Doors had 'surrendered today to Bureau Agents'. The LA office asked Miami to forward their papers to the US Marshal. They also asked other local authorities to pass on Jim's warrants to Sergeant James D. Price of the Fugitives Detail at LA's Sheriff's Office. The Sheriff (Pete Pitchess) was a staunch Republican and former FBI agent.

When the legal paper chain got rolling it couldn't stop in a hurry. In the Sunshine State's capital of Tallahassee, the supposedly 'dynamic' young governor Claude Kirk only managed to sign a warrant on April 18th '*to demand the surrender of the said James Morrison as fugitive from justice...*'[6] In other words, the rush to nail Jim Morrison was so hot that the singer turned himself in two weeks *before* his fugitive designation was officially recognized at State level. On April 24th, the day after Kirk's office released the warrant, the Assistant US Attorney Michael J. Osman announced that Morrison would no longer be prosecuted on a fugitive charge. Five days later Commissioner Swan in Miami acknowledged the federal case against The Doors' singer had been dismissed. He told the Bureau's Miami office the news on May 1st. The FBI's diligent leader would not be pleased.

After a fortnight of further procrastination, Hoover's prodigy Kenneth Whittaker informed Washington that Jim Morrison, file 511 448F, had managed to wriggle off the hook.

That ended the singer's moment of infamy as an FBI fugitive. For one long, nerve-wracking week Jim Morrison had been a fugitive from justice. Two months after his episode at Dinner Key the case was a now local matter again. He would be a free man until the Miami hearing. Or so he thought.

6
Phoenix Rising

Morrison may have escaped the fugitive charge, but Hoover and the team couldn't forget him. During the week he had been categorized an 'unlawful flight to avoid prosecution', but the FBI's main weakness was a lack of identification material. Even though Attorney Osman had dropped the federal case against James Douglas Morrison on July 11th 1969 – close to the time Elektra released *The Soft Parade* – agents at the FBI's LA office sent a 'disposition sheet' about Jim to Miami and to the Identification Division in Washington. The FBI was covering all bases; waiting on the singer's every move. Four months later they got a fresh opportunity.

Bill Siddons and Rich Linnell of West Coast Promotions scored a coup by organizing a gig for the Rolling Stones in Phoenix, set for November 12th. They gave Jim front row tickets; he, Frank Liscandro, Doors' publicist Leon Barnard and a friend called Tom Baker all went together.

The Doors felt competitive against other bands. After Mick

Jagger met the group and saw them play the Hollywood Bowl in '68, he had the audacity to tell reporters that Jim's performance was boring. Now Morrison could upstage Jagger by giving away free front row tickets at the entrance to the Veterans Coliseum…

Just before the Phoenix trip Morrison had to clear up an outstanding legal matter over in Florida. At first Max Fink thought Jim's Miami case might not get as far as the courts. Shrewdly, he called up an old pal who owed him a favour and had become a close friend of California's Republican governor, Ronald Reagan. Fink's friend said Reagan would cancel Morrison's extradition and secure a full pardon. Jim couldn't stop smiling.

As it turned out, the euphoria was short lived. During his Hollywood acting days in the early 1950s Reagan became an FBI stool pigeon. Infiltrating the Screen Actors Guild, he used his position to shop potential communists and even made a secret appearance in front of the Un-American Activities witch-hunt. His nepotistic, law-bending powers suddenly failed once he knew about Morrison's record and reputation.

Reagan sent Fink an apology; he saw no way to help Jim. So on November 9th 1969 Morrison travelled to Miami again and turned himself in at the Dade County Public Safety Department. They 'arrested' him at 9.50am and held him for just twenty minutes, during which time he entered a plea of 'not guilty' at a preliminary court session. The judge set a date for April 27th 1970 (although in the event they postponed it until August). Jim was then set free on $5,000 bail. After that he needed to return to California. The Phoenix trip two days later began in the same way as many of his frequent journeys across America.

Jim had been drinking again, this time with his buddy Tom Baker. The twosome first met in February 1967 when Pam bought a dark, clean-shaven guy along to see The Doors headline at Gazzari's down on the Strip. Thomas Frederick Baker sported curly brown hair, had a slight scar across the nose and spoke with an Irish accent. His only moment of glory came when he landed the lead in Andy Warhol's black and white epic *I, A Man*. Baker became a regular friend of Jim's early in 1968, accompanying him on drinking binges while The Doors made *Waiting for the Sun*.

Tom really saw himself as a director. Everybody else branded him a loser - Jim's shadow. He had a reputation for being arrogant and vindictive - a real jerk. Together he and Morrison made a sort of white-knuckle duo, a pair who might end up anywhere - in the slammer, in an asylum, or maybe dead – after riding their escalating exchange of schoolboy taunts and dares downhill fast.

Both men also made moves on Pam at different times. Despite being three years younger, a more talented Morrison kept up the artistic success that Baker never maintained. To get even, Baker would pick away at Jim's weak spots. He was a bad influence; when he accompanied Jim to the USC performance of *Paradise Now*, Morrison mentioned starting a riot or fire.

Everybody could see it plain as day except for Jim: Tom Baker was the sort of friend he just did not need. Yet Morrison paid Baker's expenses for the Phoenix trip. Perhaps one reason for their friendship was that Jim needed a bar room accomplice. His band-mates rarely drank with him and a man can feel so guilty staring into his glass all alone.

They boarded Continental Airlines Flight 172 on the day before the Stones' show, and true to form, Jim Morrison and his team had already been drinking. Baker sat one row behind Morrison on the other side of the aisle. By the time the plane touched down two and a half hours later, Morrison and Baker's rowdy behaviour got them both arrested. Captain Craig Chapman even came down from his cockpit twice to investigate the fuss. He radioed Continental's airport security in Phoenix at 7.00pm and did so again fifteen minutes later, asking the airport to contact the police.

When the exit door finally opened and they saw cops coming to meet them, Baker jumped up immediately, flashed his blue eyes round the cabin and shouted the *begorrahs* about how he didn't do a thing. Both he and Morrison wore bell-bottoms. Both were obviously intoxicated. Baker dressed sloppily and, as an officer noted, Jim needed a shave.

After searching the men, City of Phoenix police removed what appeared to be a long knife from Tom Baker. They handcuffed Jim and Tom in full view of everyone, and took down the names of several passengers as potential witnesses. The rumbled pair were then led down the gangway.

Leon and Frank went ahead to the Veterans Coliseum to inform the Doors' manager Bill Siddons about what had happened. Meanwhile, the City of Phoenix police kept Morrison and Baker on a 'drunk hold'. Both men declined to be interviewed. Being unsure about who might have jurisdiction over an airborne incident, at 7.40pm the police telephoned the FBI's Phoenix field office.

FBI agents arrived at the guard's office in Phoenix City jail at 10.23pm and read Baker his rights. He asked the agents to contact LA and inform Max Fink, but the Phoenix police said they had already notified the attorney. Jim was read his rights just under an hour later and the two men prepared themselves for a night in the cells.

Flight 172 went beyond Phoenix to El Paso and finally to Houston. It was due in there at around 11.37pm. Immediately after Bureau agents spoke to Morrison, the Phoenix office sent duplicate teletypes to Washington, LA and Houston. Phoenix agents requested Morrison and Baker's identification details from Washington, asked for the pair's criminal records from LA, and hoped that agents in Houston would intercept any crew or passengers leaving the aircraft. They wanted witnesses.

Having sobered up the next morning, Morrison and Baker appeared in front of a magistrate who charged them with being drunk and disorderly. He marked December 2nd as the trial date for that particular misdemeanour. Each was then asked for $66 bail money. Next, at 2.30pm the twosome were taken by 'government automobile' to appear before a US Marshal who re-booked them in front of a hastily convened federal grand jury. At 5.13pm that afternoon the Phoenix FBI informed Hoover, Los Angeles and Houston that Morrison and Baker had been indicted.

Captain Chapman charged the pair with 'intimidation of a flight crew' - exactly the same federal category used to nail hijackers. It carried a maximum penalty of $10,000 or, more worryingly, *ten years* in jail. Each harassed stewardess could file one count, and each count consisted of three felonies: assault, intimidation and threat to a member of the crew. The unthinkable notion of a whole decade behind bars soon cured Morrison's hangover.

Agents prepared to release the diabolical duo - with three counts each now under their belts – as Judge William D. Copple set the hearing for Monday 24th of November. The court demanded $2,500 bail a piece, but Fink tried to get it reduced. Nobody would budge so Siddons paid the money from a suitcase full of cash that he had accumulated from the gate at the Stones' gig! Judge Copple said Morrison and Baker could return to California but not leave the State. Altogether, Jim had spent over eighteen hours in custody.

Hoover did amazingly well out of his Establishment foray into pop culture. In the early days he caught the public interest and gave the FBI a pristine reputation, without revealing the Bureau's reality. The agency's eminence could be used to swell both its budget and its ranks. And its public prestige reflected back on the chief. Hoover gained an awesome profile as the defender of American freedoms. He was famous. The Bureau's public credibility reached a plateau in 1935 when James Cagney starred in the film *G-men.* In a national survey the next year, schoolboys voted J. Edgar Hoover the second most popular man in the country (behind Robert Ripley of *Ripley's Believe It Or Not* fame). He could be found hanging out at the Stork Club in New York City with film stars and other celebrities, signing autographs and greeting enthusiastic teens. He rode in the back of a limousine and went to all the top parties. The FBI's rugged director dressed in a pinstriped suit just like a rich mobster and he lived like an oriental potentate. A Bureau laboratory custom-made his heated toilet seat; like every other luxury, of course, it was purchased at the taxpayers' expense.

Edgar Hoover wisely maintained the source of his privilege; the Bureau's perfectionist chief continued his war on popular culture through best-selling books and more films. A quarter of a century after *G-men* another Bureau movie called *The FBI Story* appeared. Then in 1965, while Jim Morrison caroused and studied in film school, ABC TV presented their new series, *The FBI.* Five years later, although the Bureau still only retained jurisdiction over a tiny fraction of crimes (and an even smaller percentage of America's 400,000 law enforcement staff), Hoover's reputation as the nation's silhouette crime fighter remained unmatched. After four decades of leadership, his organization's budget expanded from $2 million to over $300 million per year. Its field staff total doubled twenty times over. The Bureau's commanding image was its director's lifelong achievement. And every low-down felon that the Bureau could lay its hands on, counted towards that image.

On the same day that Morrison and Baker were bailed from Phoenix, things got exciting back at the local FBI office. Houston forwarded its witness statements. The interviewees remembered a lot but said they didn't know the subjects' names. Then came a teletyped revelation straight from J. Edgar Hoover in Washington. Marked 'urgent' it stated:

> `Morrison may be identical to James Douglas Morrison, FBI number: five one one four four eight F. Similar description. Same birth date.`

At last, the FBI had put two and two together. Miraculously, they now had another chance to work on their pet hate: a radical popular performer. Being an interstate offence, crime on board an aircraft clearly came under the FBI's remit, and they pursued the case to the maximum. Most of Jim's file relates to the Phoenix case. They saw another chance to nail Jim Morrison, to string him up as the hideous role model Hoover thought he represented. This time the Bureau did their utmost to get their man.

The next day, November 13th, the FBI's Phoenix office got busy, sending sixteen copies of their memo out to just about everyone. They wanted full details of Jim's arrests in LA, Miami and New Haven. Phoenix also sent photographs of Morrison and Baker to jog the memories of witnesses in Houston. In return, Houston sent a separate dispatch that included the flight crew's addresses.

A week later, on Thursday November 20th, a Washington Capital News Service press release detailing the affair came up on the printer in Hoover's office. He put it in Jim's growing file. A new case was coming together against Jim Morrison.

7
A Singing Killer?

Assistant US Attorney Lawrence Turnoff coordinated the judicial enquiry. Turnoff wanted information on Morrison and Baker's personal backgrounds and arrest histories. The FBI gathered much of it through their LA field office. Hoover also requested Jim's arrest records from New Haven and Miami, along with an update on preparations for the Florida trial.

LA soon found Morrison's criminal record. Previously, except for Miami, Jim came off relatively unscathed from ten (!) separate tangles with the law.[1] The most famous occurred late in 1967. When The Doors were touring their second album, *Strange Days*, Jim became the first rock star to be busted on stage, just forty-eight hours after he turned twenty-four years old.

New Haven in Connecticut had a tradition of cultural intolerance. Back in 1955, police chief Francis McManus banned rock'n'roll from the city. Later, as the first chapter mentioned, local officers brought The Living Theatre to trial after *Paradise Now* cascaded beyond Yale. On the evening The Doors played

Connecticut, one uptight cop's mission to clear the backstage area was curtailed when he found Jim and a female friend in a shower stall. Mistaking the insolent lead singer for a Doors fan, the officer sprayed mace on Morrison. Local police allowed the show to go ahead only after a Doors' representative pleaded with them. Jim was physically hurt and absolutely seething.

After asking the audience if they wanted more, Jim shouted, '*Turn off the lights!*' During *Backdoor Man* he hollered, '*The whole world hates me!*' Then, once the singer explained to the crowd what happened back stage, Lieutenant Kelly stepped up to arrest him. Morrison seemed nonchalant: '*Say your thing, man.*'[2] He shrugged his shoulders and bugged his eyes like a frog, as if to ask what he had done. And they led him away to get bruised and beaten by the same cops who charged *him* with breach of the peace, indecent and immoral exhibition, and resisting arrest. He came out on $1,500 bail and although New Haven's Upstanding fined Jim $25 for the first offence, those other charges were all 'no-crimes crimes'; they never stood up.

On the bright side, the police had also unknowingly arrested three representatives of the press (including the *Life* journalist Yvonne Chabrier), so The Doors got some good write-ups. Jim only missed the cover of *Life* magazine because Martin Luther King's assassination was a more important story. An eight-page article commented on the group's rough treatment.

Because The Doors got sympathetic press, New Haven never harmed their popularity. After all, Jim didn't start anything. And if some haemorrhoidal blue-suit from *Stepford Wives* country could do *that* to somebody they assumed was a defenceless fan, what were the police coming to? In reality the New Haven incident only raised Morrison's public credibility.

Except for Miami, at the time of the Phoenix incident Jim's previous arrests were local matters all of which were already resolved. FBI records on Morrison and Baker showed 'neither subject wanted according to Identification Division files.'

In Bureau publicity material J. Edgar Hoover would proudly explain:

> The FBI is strictly a fact-gathering agency, responsible, in turn, to the Attorney General, the President, the Congress, and, in the last analysis, to the American people. The investigative and adjudicatory processes simply do not belong to the same organization.[3]

Yet the FBI exceeded their fact-gathering mandate. All the time they were waiting on the outcome of Morrison's case with a salivating sense of expectation. Jim knew the stakes:

> '*We were trying to get this erased because it's not good to have something like that on your record, man. It's just that if something really serious happened* [like the upcoming Miami trial] *you'd have a record and it makes you look a lot worse... They were trying to hang me because I was the only one that had a well known face or something, so basically they were trying to get me for it.*' [4]

The Bureau needed witness statements for the Phoenix case. Eleven first-class and fifty second-class passengers stepped off Flight 172 in Arizona, along with two 'non-revenue' cabin staff. Then in El Paso, Texas, one further first-class and three second-class passengers left the plane, together with three more non-revenue travellers. The FBI's El Paso field office was briefed to look for witnesses.

El Paso is a kind of crime port; a gateway for drug-runners crossing the Mexican border. Consequently it is also an unlikely hub of much FBI activity. Agents in the El Paso field office proved super-efficient in securing statements from three out of the five Flight 172 passengers that 'deplaned' there. These three were actually the non-revenue passengers: Continental's own employees.

It turned out that Morrison and Baker failed to appear for their 24th November hearing at the Phoenix District Court. The Doors were busy in LA recording *Morrison Hotel* at Sunset Sound studios. Judge Copple ordered Morrison and Baker to appear on December 1st. Four days later the FBI filed a report, headed 'Crime Aboard Aircraft - Assault - Interfering with Flight Crew' it noted that the head office wanted Phoenix to keep the boss updated on Assistant US Attorney Turnoff's progress; Hoover remained interested in Jim Morrison.

The Bureau's efforts take on a different hue when you realise that one upper-echelon FBI agent became infamous in the 1960s for regularly getting drunk and causing problems aboard aircraft.

On December 16th 1969 the Phoenix field office sent out a memo and witness-reports to inform not only Lawrence Turnoff, but also the Federal Aviation Authority. The FAA had independent powers to start prosecution; Hoover's men were sending out ripples, making sure Morrison got his due.

Lawrence Turnoff set the trial date for February 17th 1970 and the FBI's Phoenix office began looking to find two extra witnesses. Working with a vigilante Continental Airlines security officer they soon found them. The Bureau now had five witnesses altogether. Turnoff just needed to piece together reports of what happened on Flight 172. The race was on.

All accounts corroborated on a few scores. Morrison and Baker boarded the plane along with everyone else ready for take-off at 4.45pm. Baker settled in seat 3B and Jim sat across the aisle one row in front: seat 2C. They smelled of booze and their eyes looked bloodshot. The fourth witness said the pair 'appeared to be drunk or at least 'high". Due to an initial mechanical difficulty, the plane could not depart for about half an hour. Morrison and Baker grew impatient and wandered about in the aisle when they knew there would be a delay. As a lady sitting directly behind Baker observed, Morrison smoked a small cigar in an act of defiance during take-off at 5.10pm.

When the stewardess asked them to repeat her oxygen mask instruction, Tom Baker quipped in a voice loud enough for everyone to hear, 'My girl has one of those and she calls it a diaphragm!'

During the flight the two men smoked cigars and drank from their own spirits bottle under cover of a comic book. Baker kept saying, '*Let me see the comic book*,' as they passed it back and forth across the aisle. Flight staff found the bottle in a lavatory afterwards and passed it over to the airport police. The bottle contained a residue of Napoleon's favourite drink - Emmanuel Courvoisier's fine cognac. One and a half centuries after Napoleon, Courvoisier was Jim's favourite brandy too.

Beyond the Courvoisier, Morrison and Baker accepted those little, complimentary bottles of Chivas, Irish Cream and whatever else was going. Once both men were well oiled, the fun could begin. Tom seemed to make more trouble after he knew the plane had left the ground. The third witness said - about behaviour that appeared uncharacteristic, at least compared to Jim's public image - '*that the individual named as Baker was the instigator of the disturbance and that Morrison seemed to be urging him on*.' Tom grabbed all the soap in the lavatory, tried to sell it to his fellow passengers as he returned to his seat, then dumped it in Morrison's glass. Much to Jim's annoyance the stewardess refused to get him a new drink once his own got all soapy.

Perhaps as a result, the duo kept making '*off colour hand signals*' behind the flight staffs' backs and even sticking their feet across the aisles to hinder others' progress. Soon the two drunks were walking around the cabin and smoking at the wrong time, challenging stewardesses on the subject of seatbelt safety.

Fed up with too much badgering, one Continental stewardess went out to see Captain Craig Chapman. Chapman activated the seatbelt safety sign in mid-flight, especially to trap his rebel passengers. He then considered landing in the nearest '*field*' to have the louts removed.

Once the same stewardess came back to remonstrate with the mischievous twosome, her threat to bring out the captain had no effect. Even so, half an hour into the flight, Chapman put on his hat and coat, and came down from the cockpit. He found several hard-drinking 'hippie type' passengers in first class, but did not notice their feet sticking out across the aisles. The third witness saw Morrison and Baker try to '*back talk*' the captain, until he told them to listen. He warned that if they were going to continue, he might stop at the nearest airport or even return to LA, to have them '*recovered*' by the police. Because a time-line had been crossed in the middle of the flight, it turned out that Phoenix *was* the nearest airport - about twenty-five minutes away. After Captain Chapman made his irate speech, the pair simmered down for ten minutes, but gradually they too figured-out the landing situation and went back to their old tricks.

One stewardess said that Baker slammed a lavatory door on her at about 6.15pm. A glass half-full of booze was thrown around. Once the captain returned to the cockpit he heard the stewardesses being harassed again and asked his First Officer to spy on the cabin through the peep-hole. Speaking to flight operations in Phoenix, Chapman asked ground control to put airport security on standby. At 7.00pm the captain asked them to contact the police. He wanted an escort to board Flight 172 and make arrests. Fifteen minutes later he announced he wanted to file full charges against the two passengers. Craig Chapman said he took this decision because he heard that glasses were thrown; the stewardesses seemed shaken; '*passengers had obviously taken abuse*' and he had '*formed the opinion* [that the] *passengers causing the trouble were under the influence of either alcohol or drugs.'*

Fifteen minutes later the plane touched-down. Rather than having Morrison and Baker cause trouble for another few minutes, Chapman considered stopping his plane right there on the landing strip. During the seatbelt ban as Flight 172 taxied towards the Sky Harbor, Jim and Tom stood up and took their luggage from the overhead lockers. The FBI's third witness, who always seemed ready with the harshest version of events, said the pair reached the exit door early.

Essentially Turnoff wanted to know if the stewardesses could identify Morrison and Baker individually; if the men really caused them to operate in fear; whether the duo's talk seemed intimidating or had interfered with the captain's duties. With these questions, the *general impression* of Jim Morrison - what it *felt* like to be around him - mattered as much as what he actually *did.* According to Jim's file, the federal judicial would determine the 'degree of fear instilled by the subject's actions,' and 'the dangerousness of the situation created by the subjects'. So Lawrence Turnoff was putting Jim Morrison's shady side to the test using legal scrutiny. If Jim failed, the gruesome pay-off would be a ten-year jail sentence.

There was no doubt about it: Morrison and Baker's childish pranks inconvenienced the other passengers and divided the captain's attention. They used bad language and maintained a defiant attitude. Yet the depositions hinted at a more threatening element too: something almost sinister. Despite its apparently unplanned nature, the whole Phoenix expedition had an air of fate about it.

In the past, Jim had wanted to adopt the name 'James Phoenix' and portray himself as a rascal outlaw, a mischievous, existential rebel.

Within the plastic confines of a commercial airplane, surrounded by corporate friends on a voyage across time, Baker and Morrison had entered a different moral territory. In this highly sealed, tightly organized environment they disturbed the accepted ritual with their own blunt challenges and dark offerings. Was their drunken revelry a toxic reaction to corporate America? Or a masculine, Dionysian ritual; a libation to protect them against the ingratiating hypocrisy of modern life? Perhaps it was just the type of behaviour you might expect from a pair of crazy buddies confined so high in the sky.

Witnesses felt uneasy about the presence of Baker and Morrison: these two guys went beyond irresponsible - they seemed dangerous. One stewardess said she feared for the safety of passengers. Another was frightened that the pair might injure somebody. She didn't want to go near either man. A third stewardess said that she never wanted to meet those guys ever again, or have her own name and address even mentioned for fear of reprisals. Someone overheard Baker joking with Morrison, '*Let's kill them!*' After the pilot resumed his duties, Jim fixed the woman with a devastating stare and said, '*You're really going to be sorry now baby.*' The zealous third witness said they saw police take a large knife from the curly-haired Irishman.

Effectively the judicial process traced-out a legal phantom of Jim Morrison based on his public reputation. But did freedom, for Jim, mean the freedom to murder another human being?

Back in 1967 Jim said he wanted to kill an uncooperative New York audience who came to see Simon & Garfunkle, but had to sit through a Doors' set first. When singing *The End,* Jim would also scream about murdering his father. Just six months ago, immediately after he 'surrendered' to agents at the FBI's LA field office, Jim Morrison made a film called *HWY* out in the desert at Palm Springs. Calling Michael McClure from a phone box, and without warning, Morrison casually explained that he had killed somebody. McClure recoiled in shock, unaware it was only a sick joke - and a peculiarly revealing one too?

Ray Manzarek put it down to Jimbo, Jim's alter ego: the dark, brooding and sometimes just plain wild Lizard King. Jimbo was a fat, offensive good old boy with a penchant for alcohol, a Southern frame of reference and a tendency toward self-destruction. The beast within. Perhaps Jimbo was the fool who got busted in Miami. He could also be cold and callous, just like the hitchhiking maniac of *HWY*. But a killer? Did Morrison really have the capacity to be *a singing killer??*

'You're really going to be sorry now baby'…

According to Patricia Kennealy, '*Jim never laid a hand on me in physical violence, but he certainly made up for it in other forms of torture.*'[5] The Doors lead singer could take people out of themselves and make them as angry as they had ever been in their lives. But the facts of Jim's biography suggest he shunned the infliction of physical pain. Unlike other late '60s artists he never publicly advocated real violence. No substantiated records exist of Jim doing other people serious physical harm, not even in anger or revenge.[6] On the one occasion they ever arrested him for the crime of battery - in Inglewood January 23rd 1966 (perhaps an episode with Pam?) – police soon dismissed the charge. Jim could not even bear to cut himself at the hand-fasting rite of his pagan marriage to Patricia Kennealy in June 1970.

Given that Jim's behaviour *may* have been criminal, he was a rare sort indeed: How many 'criminals' do you know who have a social and metaphysical project? He was more mischievous than malicious. But if Jim was reticent about bloodshed, you might be forgiven for wondering where his fearsome aura came from. If Morrison flirted with terror, what were his motives?

Childhood traumas aside, why might Jim have persisted in what Kennealy called his '*psychological terror tactics*'?[7] Take his frequent 'Human Fly' ledge-walking stunts: were they just a way to show off his excellent sense of balance, the result of a silly bet, a sermon on the importance of risk or the worthlessness of life? What if Jim planned his stunts as exercises in the removal of *his own* fear, and his guilt (fear of consequences)? In Jim's hands *Light My Fire* went from a plea to a challenge. He led a life of pranks, refusals and perpetual ordeals; a burning up of unnecessary loyalties. As a result he constantly tested others around him.

People *were* panicked by Jim - friends rarely stood up to him and cops would get uneasy - not because of what he *did,* but because of how much he had successfully jettisoned from inside himself. Morrison could exude the guilt-free aura of a criminal in moments of tension, yet he mostly seemed just like any other quiet, articulate UCLA graduate; a scholar in love with words, a sober poet working hard at dawn…

Of course the *real* Jim was not on trial. Instead, Lawrence Turnoff - as a representative of the judiciary - tested a combination of Morrison's public reputation and his behaviour on Flight 172. But where on that journey did Jim's public image end and his actions begin? History cannot show us what kind of 'fact-gathering' techniques conjured up the FBI's witness statements.

Even if the issue of Jim's aura is put aside, holes were already appearing in the evidence; moments when onlookers' accounts contradicted one another. When agents interviewed Captain Chapman just two days after the offence, he couldn't remember which stewardess came up to see him first, or even what Baker and Morrison were wearing. Witnesses couldn't agree on the size of the Courvoisier bottle, let alone anything else. Had Tom Baker tried to trip flight staff up as they served cocktails? Had he slammed the toilet door on a stewardess? Or was Jim to blame? Did the captain leave his seat once or twice? Even details of a pivotal incident when a glass flew across the cabin grew hazy through the filter of multiple perspectives and unclear memories. Allegedly Jim lobbed an empty glass. Or maybe Tom did it. Jim threw part of a full drink with ice against the bulkhead and yelled too, showering a stewardess and her friend. Perhaps Baker kicked the glass out of Morrison's hand? One source said *bottles* were thrown and *glasses* were broken. The fifth witness, who never saw a toilet door slammed on anyone, said nobody threw any drinks.

On one hand, the damage was already done: those 'Dirty Doors' had supposedly proved their bad reputation again. All the reports said it was a Doors' outing. On top of Miami, the rest of the band suffered more guilt-by-association, even though Baker was nothing to do with them. In fact they detested him.

The FBI had a strong case against Morrison, yet he had one chance left: maybe his lawyers could use the abundant discrepancies between onlookers' stories to get Jim off the hook?

8

Runnin' Blue

Sitting in The Doors' office on Santa Monica Boulevard on December 9th, just one day after he turned twenty-six, Jim suffered a mild nervous breakdown. His work had nothing to do with it: the band's recent sessions for *Morrison Hotel* had gone well. Jim successfully reunited with his musicians, and they looked set to eclipse the disaster of the last single, Robby Krieger's *Runnin' Blue*, which peaked at number sixty-four in the charts six months earlier.

During one particular *Morrison Hotel* session Jim arrived with two new drinking pals. One was LA's chief of police Tom Reddin. Morrison had failed to recognize the guy, but his band-mates rapidly did. Furthermore, Reddin did not realize that his new friend was Jim - Miami! - Morrison. As soon as he put the pieces together, Tom Reddin made a swift exit - perhaps afraid for his own reputation.

The Doors still seemed a no-go area.

When John Sebastian of the Lovin' Spoonful came in to play harp on the song *Roadhouse Blues*, he asked to be credited under the pseudonym of G. Puglese as he would not be publicly associated with a band of such ill repute. After all, *Rolling Stone* did a poster-cover of Jim: 'Wanted: In The County of Dade.' A film director even approached Morrison at one point offering him the lead in a brand new movie; Jim would play a disgraced rocker. Needless to say the singer declined. Life was bad enough without imitations from art.

Morrison was stuck. He could do very little to change The Doors' public image and just had to remain silent. His lawyers told him not to talk with journalists about the Miami case until after it finished. When he gave interviews Jim carefully avoided the topic.

Meanwhile LA began to get a little strange. Jay Sebring had been Jim's hairdresser. After somebody murdered Sebring and his friends in a ferocious attack in August, several men in suits came round to question Morrison. Trying to trace their visit he found only a mystery: the police knew nothing about their detectives interrogating any Jim Morrison over Jay Sebring's murder. In October Charles Manson was indicted for organizing that crime, but the mystery of the visitors remained. For all Morrison knew it could have been the FBI.[1]

The Bureau's director once encouraged ordinary citizens to become informants and wrote, 'The FBI is as close to every person as the nearest telephone.' That summer, when a federal court found Hoover guilty of using illegal wiretaps on Martin Luther King, the FBI director's words seemed recast as a warning. A suicidal Jim thought cops would visit again if he spoke too long on the phone to Linda Ashcroft. He became especially paranoid that authorities might listen in on him.

Always there is a fear of being followed...[2]

The almost supernatural ability of Hoover's intelligence service to prey upon its victim's own fears started to take a customary toll.

Three days before his Arizona court appearance, with the combined possibility of thirteen years in jail hanging over his head, Jim Morrison - the man with perhaps the finest sense of physical balance in California - became distinctly ungainly. He acquired a taste for the music industry's mainstay: cocaine.

> Stimulant drugs have the psychological effects of giving the user a sense of increased wellbeing, self-worth, ability, power of concentration and mental agility. After high and repeated doses, however, the individual may experience confusion and panic. He tends to become irritable and nervous. He may become aggressive or may be convinced that everyone is against him, that he is being watched or followed, or that he is in danger from enemies.[3]

Patricia Kennealy and producer Paul Rothschild, among others, also took the drug to some extent. If he used alcohol to raise courage and kill pain, now Morrison began to require something to pep up his self-esteem.

Jim's relation with Max Fink also became a little rocky. Fink slowly began to understand how insecure Jim felt. Morrison walked out of their meeting on at least one occasion. The stocky lawyer treated his client with a sense of paternal forgiveness, even though Morrison had once stolen his young lady friend.

Despite an IQ of 149 and success as a lyricist, poet and singer, Jim Morrison seriously began to question his own sanity. Following the advice of Linda Ashcroft and Max Fink, under the name of James Douglas he even visited a Los Angeles psychiatrist. But in the face of his difficulties, Jim retained a sense of humour. He sent Max a small mock-up model of prison - the title attached to it read 'Morrison Hotel!'

On December 12th, represented by Fink and counsel Craig Mehrens, Morrison and Baker pleaded not guilty to all counts at a hearing in Phoenix. The trial would begin in four months.

Keeping up his FBI duties, on January 20th 1970 the Special Agent in Charge of Phoenix sent Hoover a memo informing him that Morrison's trial would soon begin. However, the rush to nail the rock star caused sloppiness once more in the compilation of the prosecution's case. A silly mistake in the legal notes nearly exonerated the two 'hippie types'. The prosecution had called the flight 'CA 71'. That particular detail needed alteration.

Count three was also deleted by the Phoenix State Attorney's office, because the third stewardess, Sheri Woodring, stepped down. Apparently Jim brushed off Woodring's groupie advances during the flight and she resented him for it. Sometime later, when both the singer and the stewardess happened to be eating at different ends of the same restaurant, Max Fink suggested that his client should approach her. The Morrison (ahem) charm worked so well that only Reva Mills and Sherry Ann Mason now backed counts against him. But neither the judicial system nor these remaining witnesses would be giving up their claims quite so easily.

Elektra Records released *Morrison Hotel* just before Jim's Phoenix trial. Even the critics were impressed; after the unfocused excess of *The Soft Parade*, The Doors bounced back under pressure with a broody, bluesy, coherent record. Jim found himself in the position of creating a successful album (which reached number four *without* the customary scout single), while remaining subject to an on-going FBI investigation.

On March 3rd 1970 the new, superseding indictment was presented before a federal grand jury. Each of the stewardesses backed one count against each man, which said that 'while aboard an aircraft in flight… [he] did assault, intimidate and threaten… a flight crew member.' A week later the FBI's Phoenix lead reported to Hoover that Turnoff had announced a new trial, set for March 12th. Since the defence motion called for a Bill of Particulars, the lead estimated the trial date would be extended for another two weeks.

The Phoenix FBI office was correct: the trial-proper got delayed until March 23rd, when Morrison and Baker – wearing suits at their attorney's request – again entered their names and pleas. The pair waived any right to a jury trial, probably because Jim thought a jury might be distracted by his decadent image and forget his real actions on the flight.

Compared to the upcoming circus in Miami, the whole event seemed relatively low profile. For the next couple of days witnesses gave their evidence. One stewardess said she heard Baker sneer, '*Let's kill them*', but admitted it was only a 'popping off' type remark: a joke not a threat.

On March 26th Judge Copple acquitted Baker, but found Morrison guilty on the count backed by Sherry Mason. The judge set a sentencing date for eleven days later. Although Jim faced greatly reduced charges, he was now living with the reality of a $300 fine and three months in jail; a share of the symbolic justice that the FBI thought he deserved. And of course Miami was still to come.

After a few days of hard thinking, on April 1st Max Fink came in with a rescue proposal. He asked the court for a postponement so he could enter an appeal. Nine days later Fink filed his motion for a re-trial. Copple then deferred Jim's sentencing by another two weeks.

At the new hearing on April 20th, Assistant US Attorney N. Warner Lee explained that the main female witness - Reva Mills from Houston, Texas - had confused the identities of Morrison and Baker. Max Fink supplied a new affidavit she had signed to say so. Because this key prosecution witness made such a vital mistake in identification it meant Baker, not Morrison, had savagely slammed the toilet door on Sherry Mason. Jim received his much-needed judgement of acquittal.

The Phoenix case indicated the judicial process was imperfect, but could be influenced by reason. Morrison's team argued for his acquittal and it had been issued.[4] At last Judge Copple vacated Jim's sentencing date and exonerated the bail bond. Jim was off the hook.

Despite diligent efforts to prosecute him, Morrison had escaped the Bureau once more. In desperation, they played a final card. On March 9th the FBI's Phoenix office informed the Federal Aviation Authority that it would 'follow and report the results of a prosecutive action' against the singer. In fact the FBI kept them so well informed that on the day of his Phoenix acquittal, the FAA threatened a civil suit against Morrison to recover $2,000 in damages. The threat lapsed and they never pressed charges, but Jim paid $600 in June the next year anyway, almost certainly to clear his name in readiness for his Miami trial.

Morrison may have eluded the Bureau yet again, but he hardly remained free, at least on artistic terms. Following Miami, members of the vice squad would turn up at Doors' gigs with open warrants, ready and eager to arrest him. After the recommendation from the Concert Hall Managers Association, venues also forced promoters to promise to pay $1,000 for every swearword he uttered on stage. Consequently, they would post a $5,000 bond redeemable only if the show passed a special moral scrutiny test conducted by local civic leaders. Rich Linnell of West Coast Promotions started to keep a 'clean file' of all performances passing the test, as evidence to persuade reluctant cities. Also, The Doors' business contract with promoters was altered to make the group waive their share of profits and perform for free if Jim got out of hand.

With the help of these precautions, live dates gradually picked up again. But when The Doors played the Felt Forum in Madison Square Garden, January 1970, Jim explained:

> *'I don't know if you're aware of it, but this whole evening is being taped for eternity and beyond that too. So listen, man: if you want to be represented in eternity with some uncouth language, then I hope you'll stand up on the top of your seat and shout it out very clearly or we're not going to get it on tape. Right?'* [5]

The implication was clear. Jim Morrison had pushed too far and already the Establishment pushed right back. Each night he faced judgement by the very people most likely to disapprove of his show. That 'no limits – no laws' episode in Miami cost him his artistic freedom on stage. In a legal sense, at least, Morrison's audience was now freer than he was.

9
American Boy

[George] *'What you represent is freedom... But talking about it and being it - that's two different things... Oh yeah; they're gonna talk to you, and talk to you, and talk to you about individual freedom but if they see a free individual it's gonna scare them.'*

[Billy] *Well, it don't make 'em runnin' scared.*

[George] *No, it makes 'em dangerous.*

- George and Billy in *Easy Rider,* 1969.

From his octagonal sanctum in the Bureau's Washington headquarters, seated behind a huge mahogany desk, for over half a century John Edgar Hoover remained America's unofficial leader.

And it appeared that Hoover ran a tight ship. The FBI's

unimpeachable leader became so obsessed with his unit's public image that he forced agents to take unpaid leave just to prevent overspending the annual budget. Desperate to improve the FBI's annual productivity statistics, he made agents re-categorize crimes and make extra arrests. Many were banned from taking coffee breaks, personally obliged to stay at a certain weight and strong-armed into voluntary unpaid overtime. Some were even sacked for baldness. Initially agents needed to be law graduates, but Hoover dropped the high entry requirements as recruitment drives began to fail. A growing number of resentful FBI interns left early and began to spread the word about their treatment.

According to Alexis de Tocqueville, '*What is to be feared is not so much the immorality of the great as the fact that immorality may lead to greatness.*'[1] Instead of his gonzo descendent the Lizard King, was the repressive, authoritarian FBI director the *real* monster?

'Welcome, Comrade Edgar.'

Could Hoover have been a secret communist? The question doesn't seem so absurd when one realizes that he thrived on corruption and turned out to be everything else that publicly he hated.

Outwardly a righteous defender of American public morals, he was also the nation's biggest blackmailer, deceiver and purveyor of obscene material. Condemning Martin Luther King and sacking his own agents for alleged same-sex affairs, the FBI director was reputedly gay himself. Although he told agents to raid the Panthers and quash black protest, Hoover may have inherited Afro-American blood from his family.

Comrade Edgar knew he could lead two lives: as a crime-fighting hero in public and vindictive manipulator in private. By controlling the flow of information he could hold opponents in check, scandalize popular figures and turn his enemies against one another. The system offered Hoover's victims no defence: what could be done when the deputy headmaster was also the school bully?

Hoover's tract *The Masters of Deceit* entered its twelfth printing by 1961. With chapters like 'How to Stay Free,' the text warned American citizens that outsiders posed a threat to their hard-won freedoms:

> If you value your freedom, and your children's freedom, read this book. It is a warning of the clear and present danger to your way of life... To regard communist fronts and their propaganda as foolish is to risk our freedom... As long as the American judicial system is strong and realistically recognizes the threat of subversion to our constitutional republic, their efforts will be hampered. They know that.[2]

Yet the whole thing was riddled with savage ironies.

> A little 'smear' campaign might be effective... Blackmail and threats are often part of communist tactics... Emotion should never replace reason as a weapon... Smears, character assassinations, and the scattering of irresponsible charges have no place in this nation. They create division, suspicion, and distrust among loyal Americans.[3]

It displaced the FBI's own dirty tricks and re-packaged them as the methods of others.

The book not only tried to alienate communists and glamorise law enforcement. Its surprisingly prominent subtext blocked every conceivable strand of progressive politics, including civil rights:

> Mass agitation weakens the noncommunist enemy and builds Party structure... The immediate demand tactics are also employed by the communists to find favour with Negroes, by urging the abolition of 'Jim Crow laws,' 'full representation,' and 'the fight for Negro rights.'[4]

Every ethnic union, every women's meeting, every local community group hid a potential communist cell.

> Consider the deceptive line for youth... 'Restore academic freedom' means to communists that we should permit the official teaching of communist doctrine in all schools and that we should allow communists to infiltrate teaching staff.[5]

Masters of Deceit managed to sell over two million copies bolstered by its placement in school libraries. With chapters on Marx, Lenin and Stalin, it did more to spread the gospel of communism than the Party ever could.

Hoover's tome reads like a Red horror story about the creeping emergence of a Soviet America. Yet in its paranoia, *Masters of Deceit* anticipated many of the themes of the counterculture.

> It is my sincere hope that members of the Communist Party will take the time to read this book [6]

Intended as the bulwark against a changing America, yet full of tips for would-be terrorists, *Masters of Deceit* can be read without much reinterpretation as Comrade Hoover's manifesto on the subversive joys of communism.

Hoover pocketed over $250,000 in royalties for his writing on communism. And the strange truth is that the man himself - seen on the back jacket fighting 'clear and present danger' with nothing but a telephone - only *masqueraded* as the author. FBI ghost-writers cooked up the book's moralistic, paranoid babble - not America's most audacious Master of Deceit.

By 1970 cracks already started to appear in Hoover's unshakable image. The Bureau's director hadn't kept up with a changing middle America. He began to fall out of favour when he called Martin Luther King a liar. His firm stance against women's liberation and the environmentalist movement was also proving unpopular. The FBI's relations with other law enforcement agencies sank to an all-time low. Assistant to the director Cartha DeLoach, the number three man in the Bureau, suddenly quit after years of loyal service. Hoover's world began to crumble around him. Even more desperately, he craved the destruction of others in order to maintain himself. He needed enemies to restore the Bureau's lifeblood: its public profile.

COINTELPRO had already been reinterpreted to divide and rule '60s radical groups. For instance, the director opened a file on 'Jane Fonda: Anarchist.' It wasn't long before Jim Morrison got his turn. After his Miami trial, The Doors' lead singer revealed, '*It was kind of an ordeal. I think it was really a kind of lifestyle they were going after. I don't think it was me personally. I just kind of stepped in to a hornet's nest.*'[7]

10
Words

The summer of 1970 was a time of desolation. After Altamont, Woodstock could only exist as a celluloid memory. The flower children's revolutionary impetus was decimated. The Living Theatre had disappeared into exile again. Nixon had co-opted the rhetoric of 'revolution.' In his speeches he envisaged hope and stability for a new decade at home, but also announced he had sent troops into Cambodia.

On May 2nd 1970, protest about the needless bloodshed in Cambodia turned so ugly that local leaders called National Guardsmen in to control a protest at Kent State University. Two days later the unrest escalated: 21,000 students became involved in the disturbances. When a pocket of guardsmen ran out of tear-gas and became isolated by angry teens, they climbed a mound and opened fire with real bullets. After ten seconds of terror four students lay dead and at least eight others were wounded.

Jim phoned Linda Ashcroft that day and yelled, '*Stay out of the street!*'[1] He feared for America. Edgar Hoover, on the other hand, displayed very little compassion. He told the presidential aide Egil Krogh, '*The Guardsmen used as much restraint as they could. The students invited and got what they deserved.*'[2] In fact none of the dead were militants. The lethal salvo came from just one weapon, triggered by fear.

The Kent State disturbance in Ohio left a continent in shock. Students from over four hundred universities immediately joined a sympathy strike. Jim Morrison and his fellow Doors happened to be on tour in near-by Pennsylvania. Two days before the incident, at the same time the Kent State kids were burning down their local ROTC building, The Doors were playing at the Civic Arena in Pittsburgh. Upon hearing news of the massacre the group even asked to do a special on-location performance as a way to help Kent State. Local authorities refused permission and The Doors moved on to Detroit.

Jim felt disappointed by the shootings and disillusioned too. He realised that nothing positive would come out of it and told Patricia Kennealy, '*I'm sorry those kids were killed. There's no excuse for what those soldiers did, but I just don't think things like that have much meaning overall. It's easy to be swayed by dramatic incidents but in the end what's changed? You have four dead kids and the system is stronger than ever.*'[3] Those words indicated a growing fatalism and despondency. Jim did nothing, for instance, to investigate exactly what data the FBI had accumulated about him.

Meanwhile, most of the rock press had abandoned The Doors. Jim said the public resented his band for being there after the revolution failed. And *he* was taking the rap for a misrepresentation, not a true measure of his persona. Jim told one interviewer,

> *'The trouble with all these busts is, people that I know - friends of mine - think it's really funny and they like to believe it's true, so they accept it. People that don't like me want to believe it because it's an incarnation of everything they consider evil. I get hung both ways.'* [4]

The FBI had been digging into Jim Morrison's background: his early days in Florida; his FSU college friends and associates. Preparation for the Phoenix prosecution gave agents their excuse. But although the FBI still withhold three pages of Jim's file to this day, nothing about this personal investigation exists in his released documents. Were Hoover's agents playing games once more?

At least one early associate tried to blackmail the rock star for the experiments of his youth, so Morrison felt decidedly uncomfortable with the FBI's Florida investigation. Jim's friend Linda Ashcroft reported he eventually became so paranoid that he would only use cash and never answer the phone himself. One day Jim took her down to his bank vault. Opening up a safety deposit box, he showed her a letter. J. Edgar Hoover had written directly to him, telling him to desist from public life. [5]

As if that wasn't bad enough, the Dade County police enjoyed threatening The Doors' lead singer with what might become of a 'pretty boy' like him inside Raiford jail.[6]

Conditioned by such hindrance, Jim awaited his trial like a turkey looks forward to Thanksgiving. He refused Patricia Kennealy's offer of spiritual protection, although he did consider using her as a character witness.[7] Jim also thought his own presence would make little difference to the proceedings. His coke intake continued and he talked in terms of *when*, not *if*, he would be convicted. For moral support, he considered flying out his own 'cheering section' to help in the courtroom. Although Morrison was resigned to his fate, his behaviour still ranged from slapstick to confrontational. He wasn't depressed so much as confused, and he retained a sense of humour.

In Phoenix, he arrived clean-shaven and wore a suit. Before Miami he reported:

> *'Well, it's still up in the air right now. There will probably be a big trial. I guess the best thing would be to buy a suit to make a good impression of me to the judge and the jury. A suit and a tie. What kind of suit? Kind of a conservative, dark blue suit. Not one of those paisley ties. More, instead one of those narrow ties: I'd like a great big tie with a great big knot. I think I'll get a suit and take a lot of tranquilizers. And just try to have a good time.'* [8]

The day before he flew to Miami for the prelims, Jim went out on a bender in LA, curled up in a doorway and was arrested for public drunkenness. Postponed from April, the Miami case was set to open on August 3rd. Soon it was rescheduled for a week later then put back a couple more days. Jury selection took place on August 12th and 13th, and the selected few were sworn-in the next day. Then, on Monday August 17th, the case-proper could start.

After all his talk about a tie, he arrived in gear he'd bought especially from LA: a white Mexican wedding shirt, brown cowboy boots, black jeans and a blue embroidered caftan jacket. His band dressed with similar informality.

Jim had long hair, a thick beard and looked like some chunky mountain man or Vietnam vet. At a time when everyone took hair as a political statement, in a city where according to Norman Mailer a few months earlier, '*You could not picture a Gala Republican who was not clean-shaven by 8.00am*,' Morrison just let it flow.[9] He remained a surly wild animal of a man, tense under the prospect of captivity.

Miami began so distressingly, in fact, that the poet-singer who once said he had an '*instinctive knack for self-image propagation*' uncharacteristically refused to face reporters as he approached the Metropolitan Dade County Justice Building for a first day in court.[10] At just twenty-six, he looked more like a tired forty. According to Patricia Kennealy, '*to my mind, what happened as a result of Miami is one of the chief contributory factors to Jim's death.*' [11] The Doors' publicist Diane Gardiner put it more succinctly: '*Jim died of old age.*' [12]

The Doors' singer's only lifeline was a written attempt to turn fate into art, to resurrect himself through words, just as his hero Artaud had managed so many times in the past.

In the absence of Morrison holding a press conference, his poetry spoke its evidence by drafting in an angel to champion the fallen rocker. After Dinner Key repercussions forced Jim to transform his exuberant live show, James D. Morrison - the poet - emerged as an adroit social critic, regardless of how adversely it might influence his trial. In February he had publicly turned civil disobedience into a subject for poetic lament in *Peace Frog* on the *Morrison Hotel* album. After Kent State he published a pacifist poem in the *Mount Alverno Review*.

And the previous summer he gave a public reading of *American Prayer*, the poem he cared about so much that he persuaded *Rolling Stone* to print it at the end of his famous July 1969 interview. Jim also published that poem in a small booklet at his own expense. As the trial began, just before the star-defendant, arrived, a Doors' publicist named Mike Gershman handed out copies to reporters. Lines about mad men running our prisons would hardly endear Jim to his captors, and he knew it. The epic poem charted those inky recesses of the 'American night': Hoover's America.

And the writing continued. All the while Morrison read his own press coverage and, sitting at the defence table in the second floor courtroom right opposite the judge, took sly notes too. The

Doors front man jotted down so much that he filled sixty pages of notepad within four days. He planned to write up his diary as Jim Morrison's *Observations on America, While on Trial for Obscenity*. Perhaps it would be serialized in Esquire magazine. Others' words contributed to this particular wound. Jim thought his own might heal it. He was, after all, a writer. The *Miami Herald* had already decided that he would be remembered for one evening of desperate vulgarity rather than a lifetime's poetic quest. The press still saw him only as an irresponsible clown. But the singer stood his ground as a freedom fighter. He came on as an illegitimate travelling preacher; a man who could see clearly, set himself up against authority and speak the truth…

11
Third Man

The Doors' attorneys rejected Judge Murray Goodman's initial plea-bargain for Jim to admit his guilt in exchange for a reduction of his charge to misdemeanours (which would result in a small fine and sixty days in some minimum security hostel). They thought they could win.

Instead of making excuses for what he might have done, Jim Morrison aimed to change US obscenity laws. And the Doors' attorneys stood right behind him; they began by pleading freedom of speech – the First Amendment.

Once he knew he would be coming to Miami, true to his character Jim read Franz Kafka's *The Trial.* Later he told a journalist,

> *'I felt like a spectator, but I wouldn't have wanted to defend myself because I would have blown it, I'm sure. It's not as easy as it looks. I didn't have to testify but we*

> *decided it might be a good thing for the jury to see what I was like, because all they could do was look at me for six weeks or whatever it was. So I testified for a couple of days.'* [1]

In his prose piece *Self Interview*, Morrison argued that to take the witness stand is to confront your own mind. And that moment is very existential; you cannot retract it. When Jim finally entered the dock he soberly explained to the judge and jury that he was only exercising artistic freedom of expression.[2]

Jim's lawyers thought they could mount a legitimate freedom of speech argument. But without too much explanation, Judge Goodman immediately rejected their idea and the case moved on swiftly.

Fink then suggested in Morrison's defence that the Dinner Key singer's charges came about through political pressure: the Establishment threatened Jim Morrison for being who he was, not for what he did. In fact the police never even questioned Jim at the time of his supposed crime.

The young prosecuting lawyer, Terence McWilliams, had been left in the lurch by his seniors – Alfonso Sepe and the other prosecutor – because it looked as if Morrison might win. They pulled out and left their assistant to shoulder the case before it had even begun. Although he seemed decidedly reluctant about his job, McWilliams proved an able lawyer. He appeared in flashy suits, avoided reporters, and called no civic witnesses, in order to make sure the political line of defence would be stifled.

Next Max Fink had his team - the Doors' Miami attorneys Robert Josefsberg and David Tariff - suggest that Jim Morrison's performance did not violate cultural standards. Jim explained to one reporter,

> *'There was profanity used in the performance, but we were going to attempt to prove that it did not violate contemporary community standards in the city of Miami. To do that we were going to take the jury to see a lot of movies like Woodstock. The musical Hair was playing in town at the time and they put nudity on stage every night. They were allowing young people to go in, of any age. A lot of books were available, even in junior high school libraries, with four letter words.'* [3]

The Living Theatre had performed a date on their controversial US tour at the Coconut Grove and no one batted an eyelid.

The State of Florida reserved the services of a special prosecutor named Leonard Rivkind to attack this community standards defence, but it turned out they didn't need him. Again, Goodman would have none of the defence's argument. He seemed to have his own reasons. *Woodstock* and *Hair* were not on trial. They were a totally separate issue.[4]

As Jim summed up, '*The judge refused to allow any investigation along those lines and limited it to a criminal action.*' [5] Max Fink's elegantly reasoned pleas could not help: instead of questioning the relevance and fairness of his charges, Jim's defence team was forced to focus solely on proving his innocence. Goodman remained unmovable.

Prosecuting lawyer Terence McWilliams actually played guitar and enjoyed the Doors' music, so all his heroes testified. At one stage he rather sheepishly asked Jim to sign a copy of the band's new album. He also wrote Jim a funny, cheeky limerick about the whole event and even ended up as Morrison's go-between. When Jim wanted to buy the rights to Jeff Simon's photos, Terence McWilliams drew up the contract.

As *The State of Florida vs. James Douglas Morrison* continued, evidence from the prosecution seemed more and more contradictory. On Wednesday August 19th David Le Vine, a witness who took photos, said Jim 'might have' used vulgar language. He demonstrated Morrison's gestures in court, ironically replaying the offence. But the *Miami Herald* had in fact already passed over Vine's pictures.

One hundred and fifty shots of Jim went on display but none showed him exposing himself. 'They had thousands of photographs from many different people that were there, and there was no photograph of an exposure or anything near it.' When the prosecution tried to enter an ambiguous negative that showed nothing when clarified as a print, Judge Goodman said, '*Nice try.*'

Bob Jennings, the tall young man who filed the initial complaint, testified on Thursday August 20th and said that he witnessed Jim on parade for a few seconds. Then James Wood, who sat next to Jennings during the show, explained that *he* saw nothing at all. The prosecution moved on quickly.

Since the trial was delayed from April and August, Max Fink developed the art of exploiting inconsistencies in statements made by the same witnesses at different times. With this technique he persuaded Officer Betty Racine to admit she'd heard a tape of the show between the two trial dates. Jim explained,

> *'They bought in thirteen witnesses. Every witness was either a policeman working there that night or someone who worked for the City and happened to be there, or a relative of a policeman. In fact their biggest witness was a sixteen year old girl who was the niece of a police officer that got her and her date in for free that night.'* [6]

Between court sessions Jim stayed in room 663 of the Carillon, a medium sized hotel at the top end of Miami Beach. From there his entourage could reach the courthouse in fifteen minutes by driving across the John F. Kennedy Causeway, along Biscayne Boulevard and down into town. Jim asked Pamela Courson to stay in LA so he could recuperate in the evenings without burdening her with his frustration. Part way through the trial Patricia Kennealy, Jim's east coast lover, telephoned from New York with some troubling news: she was carrying a child. His child.

Almost immediately she flew down to Miami and the pair exchanged tense words. They stared at each other, through tears. Neither had ever faced a situation like it before. The shock pregnancy created an unprecedented mental burden. Although it could not influence the grim judicial process, it bought home the effect of that process on Jim's future. He told her, *'If this had happened at any other time things would have been very different... you want to give a baby a convict for a father?'* [7] Of course Patricia did not want to do that, or to bring up a child in extreme poverty all by herself. She underwent a ghastly saline abortion (detailed in her book *Strange Days* - Jim paid for it but did not attend) and also faced the unexpected horror of signing the baby's death certificate. Her ill-timed pregnancy exposed the price that the Establishment slowly forced Jim to pay in Miami.

All the time Judge Goodman dragged the case out. He continually postponed, cancelled, and rescheduled court. Goodman held it every other day; perhaps timing the verdict ready for his own re-election.[8] Speaking about Murray Goodman's tactics, Jim told a reporter that he never really knew from one day to the next when court was in session as the judge changed it every day.[9] Partly as a result, journalists slowly lost interest too. A local TV station constantly covered the event for the first four days but then gave up, bored by the glacial pace of proceedings. Meanwhile Morrison's trial began to cost The Doors a small fortune in flight tickets, hotel bills and legal fees. On top of all the cancellations that came directly after the Dinner Key incident itself, over thirty additional Doors' gigs scheduled for 1970 never happened because of the trial. Jim could hardly sing for the crowds; he needed each weekend to recuperate.

Judge Goodman's manoeuvres only allowed the band to earn money by playing live on two trips; one was to California and the other, the Isle of Wight festival. A lucrative European tour they had planned as a follow up to that show also had to be scrapped.

It became a cunning war of attrition. If the defendant's finances could be wasted, he would lose the means to struggle. Jim told a reporter afterwards, '*If I hadn't had unlimited funds to continue fighting my case, I'd be in jail right now for three years. It's just that if you've got the money you generally don't go to jail.*' [10] When Jim died, his estate still owed $75,000 in legal fees.

If a man's stature could be measured by the importance of his enemies, Jim Morrison would have been counted as a giant indeed. During the final years he made enemies of America's *three* most important men.

Edgar Hoover had, of course, already sent Jim Morrison a letter asking him to disappear from public life.

Richard Nixon's letter to the Orange Bowl rally showed that the president knew about the fuss over decency in Miami. Also Nixon began office as one of the few presidents on good terms with the FBI's entrenched director. In truth, Hoover considered President Nixon his own prodigy. The two men did a lot of back scratching: Hoover tutored his candidate, invited him to dinner, then institutionalized an upward flow of smear material about other people – blackmail-fodder – when the president was in office. In return Nixon never pressed for Hoover's retirement but instead gave him a pay rise and commissioned a new FBI headquarters in Washington. Work soon began on the 'J. Edgar Hoover Building' at the corner of 9th and Pennsylvania Avenue. Even though a knowing kind of tension soon held the two men at a distance, when Hoover died Richard Nixon buried his friend's obese corpse with the full honours of a national hero.

The third American leader that Jim crossed came from the other side of the tracks.

With over a thousand staff, the Fontainebleau hotel dominates the most prestigious stretch of Miami Beach. Its interior is so colossal that you can easily lose people there, and so luxurious it became the set for James Bond's playboy espionage in *Goldfinger*.

The Fontainebleau also hosted Nixon's Republican triumph just two years before Jim Morrison found himself there during his Miami prosecution. Morrison's magnetism got him into trouble again when Fink took him along to a swank dinner party. Jim just wanted something to do to take his mind off the trial. The Doors' singer stood out against his glamorous new surroundings, the only casually dressed man in a crowd of middle-aged black-tie sorts. Later that evening he left with a blonde who turned out to be trouble. She was the moll of an infamous Mafia gang lord.[11]

Despite their traditional face of upstanding morality, the streets of Miami have always hidden a very different story. As a port gateway the city was in reality the biggest vice den east of Las Vegas. From the mob condominiums of Miami Beach to Little Haiti's squalid gang lands, it concealed a rotting underbelly of drugs, gambling, loan-sharking, racketeering, kickbacks and prostitution. The city became an incongruous mix of public wealth and private vice, a place where the local arm of the Establishment was paid to turn a blind eye. Even the diminutive Judge Goodman got arrested a year after Jim's trial on bribery charges following a gambling case – although they acquitted him. In fact Miami maintained a City government so corrupt that thirty years later locals introduced a referendum to abolish it.

South Florida's sin city was not only a favourite haunt of Edgar Hoover; it was also the home of Meyer Lansky.

Maier Suchowljansky, a.k.a. Meyer 'The Little Man' Lansky,

became the exception that proved the rule of organized crime. As co-founder (together with Charles 'Lucky' Luciano) of the Mafia's forerunner organization - the National Crime Syndicate - Lansky was arguably the most important mob leader in America. In comparison 'Lucky' was decidedly unlucky: he got put away in 1936 and died in 1962. Lansky remained a free man. Despite his non-violent reputation, the honorary Italian (who was actually an erudite Polish Jew) not only ordered the killings of his competitors; he also dispatched his wayward friend Bugsy Siegel. 'The Little Man' became so notorious in Florida that locals gave his patch near the Hallandale racecourse the title 'Lanskyland.'

As it happened, in 1970 the Miami judicial machine also summoned Meyer Lansky. He faced felony and misdemeanour charges for whatever mob-chasing government investigators could throw at him - income tax fraud and even possession of household drugs without a prescription.

Consequently in the middle of his own trial, Jim Morrison had completely by accident seduced the fancy woman of America's most important crime boss. And that pair's chance meeting at the Fontainebleau didn't go unnoticed. Lansky's henchman rang up Max Fink and told him to pass on a painful message. The mob threatened Jim Morrison with serious violence, but he remained quite cool about it and even appeared to enjoy the intrigue. He went out with the lady again. Who can believe the brazen indifference of the condemned?

Meyer Lansky had a reason to hate Morrison - could he, Hoover and the President have formed an unholy alliance to seal the singer's fate through downward pressure on the judiciary? Potentially, since it emerged as a common interest at the top. Furthermore Lansky had the connections.

While they carefully avoided speaking to each other in public, Lansky and Hoover frequented the same Miami restaurants. Both dined in places like Joe's Stone Crabs - a pushy, overpriced joint on the tip of South Beach – but they never spoke. The two fading leaders were locked in an intriguing standoff.

To the general public, Hoover's sexuality was a mystery. Back in the late 1920s local police had him arrested in a New Orleans toilet on sex charges involving another young man. Later, by obtaining some compromising photos of Hoover and his lifelong friend Clyde Tolson (a mean-eyed and petite character always trailing behind the boss's commanding stride), Lansky played America's tough-talking crime fighter at his own game: blackmail. Shanghaied into silence, Hoover went unusually quiet when organized crime was mentioned and did all he could to keep the heat off mob activities.

The Bureau once ignored a disgraced member of the Buffalo 'family' named James Delmont who walked into their Miami field office with some juicy information. Less than a year later Delmont died, the victim of a classic Mafia hit in Los Angeles. The FBI in Miami said they had no record of his visit. Despite a field staff of over a hundred and fifty agents, nobody knew anything. Perhaps they'd been too busy chasing rock stars.

To keep everything sugar-coated, Lansky's heavy Phil 'The Stick' Kovolick would deliver winning numbers to Hoover's special table at the Hialeah racetrack. In exchange for the Bureau turning a blind eye, the Mafia gave its director tips on fixed races: that way Hoover could pick up his perks. No evidence of bribery remained. Edgar even boasted about his gambling exploits to Robert Mardian, an Assistant Attorney General during the Nixon administration. With almost mystical powers of prediction, the FBI director made fat wagers and always won.

So at the same time that Hoover was manufacturing a Red peril he dismissed the existence of the Mafia. Although Bobby Kennedy's spell as Attorney General for six years from 1957 onward forced the Bureau to step up its fight against organized crime, since then they'd slackened off again. Hoover didn't want his agents tainted by the risk of Mafia bribery (although he seemed happy enough to take it!). In his absence other government agencies pursued Lansky's case.

Morrison's different enemies didn't even need to discuss him. It turned out that all the corrupt networks of Florida's crime capital were unnecessary. Afraid of an unkind judge, Morrison opted for a jury trial. But Judge Goodman ignored indications from the Orange Bowl teens and made sure none of the jurors were below the age of thirty. Jim's *trial by jury* meant that *locals* decided his future - locals who had, undoubtedly, already absorbed the prolonged media fuss about The Doors.

12
The End

On the last day of the trial, September 19th 1970, Morrison's lawyers cleared the court and asked that Judge Murray Goodman admit a further twenty-eight sworn witness statements as evidence that Jim didn't expose himself. Jim told those around him that he never actually exposed himself, but with Goodman's attitude what difference would it make?

Goodman simply said, '*Gentlemen, you've proven that Mr. Morrison didn't expose himself. I'm not going to allow this evidence, to save time.*' [1]

Jim explained to a journalist,

> '*The judge limited the defence's witnesses. We had three hundred witnesses who were there. We were going to parade them all in to get their side of it. He limited the defence to the number of witnesses that the prosecution bought on, which is an entirely arbitrary manoeuver. But we had three hundred people that were willing to testify that they were*

> *there and didn't see anything - any of those alleged incidents.'* [2]

As the jury filed back in, Murray Goodman *never told them* his opinion that Jim was innocent. While the Doors' attorneys bombarded the gathering with over three hours of summing up, McWilliams took just under fifteen minutes. Then, after deliberating for over two hours on Saturday night and finishing with a shorter meeting on Sunday, the jury announced their decision.

The guilty verdict was in.

In a surprising inversion of the expected outcome, the local jury – all middle-aged and only half the size of a traditional twelve person team - found Jim Morrison guilty of indecent exposure and profanity, but not drunkenness, gross lewdness or lascivious behaviour. In other words, they thought he'd exposed himself, but not in a vulgar or obscene way.

Fink immediately filed an appeal claiming judicial prejudice and the denial of freedom of speech.

Judge Goodman demanded a whopping $50,000 bail from Morrison *in cash*, but agreed to another type of payment when the Doors' attorneys complained. Now all Jim could do was to wait for his sentence.

When Morrison returned to LA his mood deteriorated. Pam Courson left him and went to Paris following an argument that erupted between them. She knew a rich count living there.

After the deaths of Jimi Hendrix on September 18th and Janis Joplin a few weeks later, depressed and drinking again Morrison told his friends they were looking at Number Three. He felt his days were numbered.

The Florida legal system contains an official cash bargaining system that permits a trade of marginal or unsteady convictions for money. If the client is rich the court at least gets something out of the deal. At different points in the prosecution, Judge Goodman exercised his prerogative and offered Max Fink deals in exchange for cash. To help sweeten Jim's sentencing Fink eventually paid Goodman off as requested, but he only gave the judge a fraction of the sum asked for. The lawyer had confidence in a positive outcome, or at least the likelihood of a successful appeal.

Case number F69 2355 against James Douglas Morrison, opened on March 5th 1969, and came to an end on 30th October 1970.

As Jim put it, '*First of all they never really proved anything except for profanity, which we admitted all along... And the other charges I think were put there to make it look more serious.*' [3]

Meanwhile all the charges were *dismissed* against Meyer Lansky - a real gangster with a cool $300 million personal fortune – and he flew off seeking asylum in Israel. Morrison awaited a grim fate for his victimless crime. He later told a reporter, '*I think before the trial I had a very unrealistic schoolboy attitude to the American judicial system and my eyes have been opened up a little bit.*' [4] When Judge Goodman explained to Fink that additional payment would buy Jim a suspended sentence, the lawyer refused to play ball. Instead he made a special plea for mercy on Jim Morrison's behalf. Max said that Jim, whom he'd known for several years, was a good man who made an artistic contribution to society. Judge Goodman ignored the plea.

For the two convictions, Jim Morrison faced a maximum possible fine of $525 and eight months in jail (as well as two years' probation). Relatively speaking, the fine appeared an insignificant sum for a rock star, but how much was it worth as a *symbolic* punishment? Would a fine really have mattered to Jim? At gigs he introduced John Lee Hooker's *Money* as America's national anthem. He gave away $100 bills and didn't own a house or even carry a wallet. After he crashed his Shelby Cobra, Morrison even rented his cars. How could a relatively small fine have meant very much to him? Jail, on the other hand, was a different matter.

In front of a courtroom packed with media representatives, Judge Goodman told Jim, '*You are a person graced with talent and admired by many of your peers. Man tends to imitate that which he admires and those gifted with the ability to lead and influence others should strive to bring out the best, and not the worst in admirers.*' [5] The judge gave no evidence for his assertion - no copycat cases to back up his statement. But he loaded Jim up with a sentence close to the maximum possible: six months of hard labour for indecent exposure, another sixty days (to run concurrently) for profanity and a $500 fine.

Morrison said before his trial, '*They're gonna crucify me!*' [6] Now it seemed he was right.

The Establishment won the day. Prison contradicted Jim Morrison's entire project. Confinement was suddenly more than just a threat; it was an expectation.

Elmer Valentine and Phil Tanzini once threw Jim out of the Whiskey in the early days for an unexpectedly oedipal romp through *The End.* Although he had always unnerved such people, Morrison never really cared. He would shrug off their reaction as the predictable result of his own little joke. People were out of tune with his mischievous sense of humour. He loved it: '*I think we're the band you love to hate. It's been that way from the beginning. We were universally despised. I kind of relish the whole situation.*' [7] But in Miami the newspapers blew up his bad reputation and lobbied for his arrest. Now they treated Jim himself as a joke, ignoring his fight to clear his name and liberate stage performance. In contrast the judiciary took him all too seriously.

Back in 1965 Jim confessed to Ray that he didn't feel grown up. After the Miami trial he told a reporter, '*I wasted a lot of time and energy on that thing, and had about a year and a half of gnawing disquiet about it. But I guess it was a valuable experience…*'[8] The ordeal in Miami matured him; he could no longer use humour as his get-out clause, but for all that gain there was also a loss. Hoover could never laugh at himself. The FBI and Florida authorities had now crushed the remainder of Jim's healthy, self-deprecating sense of humour too. Nobody accepted the jokes this time. Since the legal process might take two years to go through, if his appeal came to nothing Jim would see the inside of Raiford sometime in 1972.

During his trial, he asked Linda Ashcroft, '*Will you love me better after death?*' [9] Following the verdict, at the end of 1970 he said to Patricia Kennealy, '*What would you do if I died... Would you kill yourself?*' [10]

After finishing vocals for The Doors' masterful new album *LA Woman,* in April 1971, before his team had even mixed the record, Jim Morrison stepped onto an inter-continental flight.

Paris beckoned - the Paris of Artaud, pronounced mad; of Baudelaire on trial for obscenity; of Rimbaud's scandalous affair and May '68 - a lyrical Paris of the mind. Jim carefully calculated his journey from the City of Angels to the City of Light. Unbeknown to anyone, he would never see his cherished Los Angeles again or the rest of his vast native land. In America they still categorized him a criminal.

The Doors decided not to publicize their singer's European excursion. Ray Manzarek wondered how Jim could escape detection when he left the country. Of course the business of tracking felons is more sophisticated today, but the Bureau kept Jim's identification on record at their National Crime Information Centre - a system that had already operated for four years. And if the FBI deemed further intelligence gathering necessary, they could always have contacted their Paris field office. Around five hundred agents were available to comb the streets of the city. But in truth there was no need to keep a tight rein on Morrison. Judicially the Bureau had him right where they wanted him. Why bother to keep tabs? Jim even visited Morocco towards the end of April.

Free from the band's commitments, from the pressures of the American justice system, and free even from his old drinking buddies, Jim grew used to watching the world from his seat at the Café de Flore. Existence in the sleepy, aristocratic Marais district offered its own rewards. Pam found a modest apartment on the rue Beautreillis, not far from the Place de la Bastille with its tall July Column - a reminder that the city achieved freedom.

Refreshed by the energy of Paris life, Jim Morrison began to write again.

But his efforts were erratic. He still experienced mood swings. In June, he sent a letter to Patricia Kennealy. She recalled, '*The pages seemed frosted with hopelessness*'; Morrison felt unable to find his voice as a writer.[11] Then again, the show business and music offers never stopped coming. Jim thought about returning to the USA in July or September. But despite another top five Doors' album he was non-committal about continuing with the group. Their 1968 Amsterdam gig hinted that audiences might support The Doors without him. In Jim's absence his band-mates began to audition other vocalists. Then they heard the news: Jim Morrison was dead.

13
Interested in Freedom

July 3rd 1971.
Estimated time of death: 5.00am.
Cause: heart failure.

It could hardly have been suicide if Jim's last words were really: '*Pam, are you still there?*' [1] More likely he snorted some of his girlfriend's heroin. Maybe - since Jim always claimed he detested that stuff - he mistook it for cocaine.

> The traditional sign of narcotic overdose is that the pupils of the eye are reduced to pin point size... Body temperature is low, and the skin may be quite cold. The victim's body will be limp and relaxed, and his tongue may be lying in the back of his throat blocking his air passage.[2]

Representatives of both the local police and fire departments reported Jim Morrison was found in the bath tub, bleeding from the left nostril, turning the water pink as the dawn.

In a way the event wreaked of destiny. Jim's lifelong experiment to transcend the dark recesses of America came to an end in Paris, the City of Light. His life proved an inspiration and in death he left behind a mystery. The singer was buried among the bones of poets in a bygone corner of Paris, stray cats slinking across his grave. Right to the end, it seems, he remained on the edge - still looking for comfort in chemicals, perhaps worried about those six months in Raiford still hanging over his head.

Five mourners were present as a polished oak box receded into the broken earth of Père-Lachaise. Jim's body rested deep between austere monuments. Stone anagrams of death in a garden of mourning. The Paris air felt surprisingly damp that balmy July day.

In lieu of a funeral service, Patricia Kennealy persuaded a local priest to pronounce the sacrament over Jim's grave.

May the angels lead thee into Paradise.

Over in Brazil, locked up again for their confrontational theatre, Julian Beck and Judith Malina heard about Morrison's untimely death from a newspaper pushed inside their cell.

Judith wept. Long ago she once said, '*In Paradise, nobody dies.*'[3]

FBI file 511 448F does not record James Douglas Morrison's passing. Instead it remains forever open; the fragments cut adrift from his turbulent life. Never actually going to jail, Jim stayed as free in death as he did in life.

On December 9th 2010, the day after what would have been Jim's 67th birthday, Governor Charlie Crist led the Florida State Board of Executive Clemency in granting a pardon for Jim's alleged exposure in Miami. Crist argued that the singer had left a significant artistic legacy, that there had never been sufficient evidence to bring the original case, and that because Jim was dead, '*In this case, guilt or innocence is in God's hands, not ours.*'[4]

Jim Morrison left without saying goodbye. But after the Miami trial he signed off with a small statement.

'*I am not mad. I am interested in freedom.*'[5]

Endnotes

FOREWORD

1. Patricia Kennealy, *Strange Days: My Life With and Without Jim Morrison* (New York: Plume, 1995), 433. Patricia Kennely (sic) united with Jim in a pagan hand-fasting ceremony. In 1979 she changed her name to Patricia Kennealy-Morrison for the sake of memory and pronunciation. I will use the surname Kennealy, as she does in her book *Strange Days*. This is for convenience and accuracy: despite his proposals, Jim never *legally* got married.

2. From The Doors' original Elektra press release, reproduced in James Riordan and Jerry Prochnicky, *Break on Through: The Life and Death of Jim Morrison* (New York: It Books), 373.

3. Ray Manzarek, *Light My Fire: My Life with The Doors* (New York: Berkley Boulevard, 1999), 324.

4. Peter Feniak, "Jim Morrison: Rider on the Storm," *Toronto Globe and Mail,* July 6, 1996, C3.

5. Kennealy, Strange Days, 16.

6. William Blake, *The Complete Prose and Poetry of William Blake* (Berkeley: University of California Press, 1995), 35.

7. Manzarek, *Light My Fire*, 124.

8. Lizze James, "Jim Morrison: Ten Years Gone," *Creem*, 1981.

9. Manzarek, *Light My Fire*, 132.

10. Ibid., 264.

11. John Densmore, *Riders on The Storm* (New York: Delta, 1990), 116.

12. Anthony Summers, *J. Edgar Hoover: Official and Confidential* (New York: Putnam Adult, 1993). Both George Washington University and NYU in New York bestowed honorary doctorates on Hoover, but in 1964 when Marquette University in Milwaukee considered giving King an honorary degree, FBI agents - the same people Hoover loved to call courageous and self-sacrificing men - paid a visit to change their minds. In 1964 FBI

representatives also tried to dissuade the Pope from granting King an audience. Back in the USA, in front of a pack of journalists Hoover called the black leader the most notorious liar in the country. Between clenched teeth, King said in reply that Mr. Hoover had apparently faltered under the awesome burden, complexities and responsibilities of his office. After that the Bureau hounded Martin Luther King at every available opportunity: eavesdropping on his private conversations, wire-tapping his telephone and sending him an intimidating anonymous tape compiled from their surveillance operation. When Hoover's campaign was revealed in the summer of 1969 it may have shaken Jim Morrison; he was an FBI concern at the time.

13. Frank Lisciandro, *Jim Morrison: An Hour for the Magic* (London: Plexus, 1993), 140.

14. Reproduced in Michel Foucault, *Madness and Civilization* (Abingdon: Routledge Classics, 2001), xi.

Chapter 1: STRANGE DAYS

1. *Signals Through the Flames*, dir. Sheldon Rochlin, 97 min., 1983, video cassette.

2. Julian Beck and Judith Malina, "Paradise Now," *Tulane Drama Review* 13, no. 3 (1969).

3. *Signals Through the Flames*, dir. Rochlin, 1983.

4. Hazel Smith and Roger Dean (1991) *Improvisation, Hypermedia and The Arts Since 1945* (Amsterdam: Harwood, 1991), 230.

5. Reproduced in Terrell Mars, "The Living Theatre: History, Theatrics and Politics" (MA Diss., Texas Tech University, 1984), 59-60.

6. Judith Malina, *The Enormous Despair* (New York: Random House 1972), 99.

7. *Signals Through the Flames*, dir. Rochlin, 1983.

8. Malina, *The Enormous Despair*, 3.

9. Ibid., 3.

10. Ibid., 133.

11. Ibid., 117.

Chapter 2: A GLIMPSE OF PARADISE

1. Author unknown, "Le Living," *Ramparts*, November 30, 1968, 40.

2. Malina, *The Enormous Despair*, 175.

3. *Signals Through the Flames*, dir. Rochlin, 1983.

4. Beck and Malina, "Paradise Now," *Tulane Drama Review*.

5. Bill Kerby, "Artaud Rock: The Dark Logic of the Doors," *The UCLA Daily Bruin*, May 24, 1967.

6. Fred Powledge, "Wicked Go the Doors: An Adult's Education by the Kings of Acid Rock," *Life* 64, April 12, 1968, 94.

7. Much doubt exists about the exact date of recording *Rock is Dead*. Some authorities place it during the *Morrison Hotel* sessions (late 1969) while others position it within the taping of the *Soft Parade* (late 1968 to mid-1969). I think the latter seems more likely.

8. *Signals Through the Flames*, dir. Rochlin, 1983.

9. Malina, *The Enormous Despair*, 193.

10. Ibid., 175.

Chapter 3: LAMB TO THE SLAUGHTER

1. The economics of the Dinner Key evening: bargained down by Siddons, Collier had already offered The Doors a $25,000 flat fee instead of the usual 60% of the gate. Their agreement was based on calculations that a 7,000 capacity hangar could gross $42,000. On the night, the promoter sold around 8,000 tickets at 50c to $1 *over* the agreed $6 cover price. Next, Collier's team removed seats in order to pack another 5,000 ticket-buyers into the auditorium. They had effectively upped the gross to $75,000 but not split the extra profits.

2. This interview was released as part of *Jim Morrison: The Ultimate Spoken Word Collection* 1967-1970, Ozit Records, compact disc OZITCD 0025.

3. Jerry Hopkins and Danny Sugarman, *No One Gets Out of Here Alive* (New York: Warner Books, 1995), 234.

4. Ibid., 311.

5. James Riordan and Jerry Prochnicky, *Break on Through: The Life and Death of Jim Morrison* (New York: It Books, 1992), 302.

6. Ibid., 297.

7. Ibid., 298. This stunning taunt comes from a political tradition that also includes Elias Canetti's pointed aphorism: 'The lives of most people ultimately consist of nothing but the directions that they senselessly give themselves or others.' To me, that sums up

exactly what Jim opposed.

8. Densmore, *Riders on the Storm*, 211-212.

9. From The Doors' original Elektra press release, reproduced in Riordan and Prochnicky, *Break on Through*, 122.

10. Manzarek, *Light My Fire*, 312.

11. Larry Mahoney, "Rock Group Fails to Stir a Riot," *The Miami Herald*, March 3, 1969, 1B.

12. Riordan and Prochnicky, *Break on Through*, 303.

13. This typically passive-voiced piece of Bureau-speak does not say *who* would contact the State Attorney. The rest of the report is blanked to avoid revealing a confidential *law enforcement agency* source. The quote suggests that either the FBI took action, or they would ensure that the Miami police did.

14. Four crimes and six warrants: 1 felony (lewd and lascivious behaviour) and 5 misdemeanours (2 for indecent exposure, 2 for profanity and 1 for public drunkenness).

15. Riordan and Prochnicky, *Break on Through*, 303-304.

16. Malina, *The Enormous Despair*, 213.

17. Ibid., 216.

18. Aldo Rostagno with Julian Beck and Judith Malina, *We: The Living Theatre* (New York: Ballantine Books, 1970).

19. Riordan and Prochnicky, *Break on Through,* 409.

Chapter 4: SOME WAY TO STOP IT

1. Kennealy, Strange Days, 49.

2. Riordan and Prochnicky, *Break on Through,* 303.

3. Author unknown, "Coliseum Ruckus Erupts During 'The Doors' Show," *Phoenix Gazette*, November 8, 1968, 1 and 4.

4. Norman Mailer, *Miami and The Siege of Chicago: An Informal History of the American Political Conventions of 1968* (New York: NYRB Classics, 2008), 42.

5. I might add here that Jackie Gleason was a big drinker. Kate Smith passionately sold war bonds – investments in death – just before Jim Morrison was born, and Levesque's own adventure ended in disaster. Three rallies later, his Decency movement

collapsed into factional in-fighting.

6. The Morrison clipping was also passed along to Robert Mahoney. Unfortunately, that meant it never ended up in file 511 448F.

7. Malina, *The Enormous Despair*, 88.

8. Tuli Kupferberg's 1997 interview with Jason Gross; available from: http://www.furious.com/perfect/tuli.html.

9. Riordan and Prochnicky, *Break on Through*, 298.

10. Lawrence Lipton, *The Holy Barbarians* (New York: Messner, 1959), 15.

11. In his *Paris Journal*, Jim suggested that something was lost when the idea of purity emerged. See Jim Morrison, *The American Night* (New York, Vintage Books, 1991), 195.

12. Interview reproduced on *The Ultimate Spoken Word Collection,* compact disc.

13. Some biographers argue that the FBI had marked Morrison as a potential threat to America after New Haven, but all the surviving evidence can *demonstrate* is that Whittaker's 4th March 1969 COINTELPRO message told Hoover about Morrison. Whether Hoover considered say, the *Life* magazine article

beforehand is hard to tell.

14. Summers, *J. Edgar Hoover: Official and Confidential.*

15. No record of this call exists on Jim Morrison's file, but the timing of the issue of his fugitive warrant leads me to surmise that contact of some kind took place. Officially the FBI do not 'take over' a case, but they form a task force with local authorities if a crime comes within their jurisdiction. In Jim's case they engineered one of these forces right from the start.

    At least one biographer has suggested that the FBI issued the fugitive warrant because Morrison showed no sign of returning to Miami. The Whittaker report (mention of felony) and timing of Edward Swan's fugitive warrant (just after the Orange Bowl, Nixon's letter of support, and Hoover's reply to Crutchfield) together suggest *the FBI* picked the moment. After all, President Nixon controlled Bureau funding via the Senate Appropriations Committee. Looking at it the other way, there is no counter-evidence yet that says the Miami judiciary got the FBI involved, or that there was anything automatic about the fugitive designation. In fact, the Swan warrant gave Jim a Tallahassee number, which indicates that preliminary connections had already been made at State level. Hoover's biographer Anthony Summers states, 'Edgar made an art form of concealing information in alternate file systems or simply not recording it at all.' See Summers, *J. Edgar Hoover: Official and Confidential*, 144.

Chapter 5: THE FUGITIVE

1. Interview reproduced on *The Ultimate Spoken Word Collection,* compact disc.

2. Riordan and Prochnicky, *Break on Through*, 315.

3. Author unknown, "James Bond Inspired Myths Will Only Confuse In Attempt to Calculate Soviet Spy Strength," *Lebanon Daily News*, July 4, 1967, 17.

4. J. Edgar Hoover, *Masters of Deceit* (New York: Pocket Books, 1961), 256.

5. Ibid., 258.

6. I obtained the date for the local fugitive warrant by looking in Jim's FBI file. The subsequent Florida State warrant can be seen here: Patricia Butler, *The Tragic Romance of Pamela & Jim Morrison* (London: Omnibus Press, 1999), 140.

Chapter 7: A SINGING KILLER?

1. Jim's crimes together with place of indictment: drunkenness / theft of police helmet and umbrella (Tallahassee, Fla. September 1963); battery (Inglewood, CA. January 1966); drunkenness (LA, CA. February 1967); various (New Haven, Conn. December 1967); vagrancy / drunkenness (Las Vegas, Nev. January 1968); drunk driving without license (LA, CA. February 1968); UFAP / lewd & lascivious behaviour (LA, CA. April 1969); lewd & lascivious behaviour etc (Miami, Fla. November 1969); drunkenness (Phoenix, Ariz. November 1969); crime abroad aircraft (Phoenix, Ariz.

November 1969)... For more details see Riordan and Prochnicky, *Break on Through*, 375.

2. Jim's words from this event are reproduced in Riordan and Prochnicky, *Break on Through*, 208.

3. Hoover, *Masters of Deceit*, 291.

4. Interview reproduced on *The Ultimate Spoken Word Collection*, compact disc.

5. Kennealy, *Strange Days*, 419.

6. I do not mean here that Jim was an angel, that he never had a drunken brawl or shook his girlfriend. He was a human being. He was an alcoholic. But, particularly in the context of his regular problems with police and the widespread discontent of his time, Morrison's *actions* seem remarkably free of significant physical brutality.

7. Kennealy, *Strange Days*, 420.

Chapter 8: RUNNIN' BLUE

1. Jim's interrogation in connection with the Manson murders is mentioned by Linda Ashcroft in her book *Wild Child* (1997, 409).

No trace of it can be found in the FBI file. However, the American government has other information-gathering agencies. Private detectives could also have been involved.

2. Drug information taken from: Canadian Department of Health and Welfare, *Bad Trips, Freakouts, Overdoses: Emergency Treatment of Drug Crises* (Ottawa: Information Canada, 1975), 31.

3. Ibid.

4. The Phoenix trial had a beneficial upshot: Baker and Morrison fell out the next day and didn't see each other for over six months afterwards.

5. Jim can be heard saying this on a track called *We Have A Special Treat [Live]* on The Doors, *Live In New York, Felt Forum*, Rhino Records, compact disc R2 521 457.

Chapter 9: AMERICAN BOY

1. Alexis de Tocquville, *Democracy in America* (New York, Vintage Books, 1990), 226.

2. Hoover, *Masters of Deceit*, 1.

3. Hoover, *Masters of Deceit*, 209. While Hoover was describing the underhand tactics of the Communists here, we know that his Official and Confidential correspondence file contained

'derogatory information' on Martin Luther King. See Athan Theoharis, *The J. Edgar Hoover Official and Confidential File* (Bethesda: University Publications of America, 1990), 6.

4. Hoover, *Masters of Deceit*, 181.

5. Ibid., 186-187.

6. Ibid., vii.

7. Interview reproduced on *The Ultimate Spoken Word Collection,* compact disc.

Chapter 10: WORDS

1. Linda Ashcroft, *Wild Child: Life with Jim Morrison* (New York: Thunder's Mouth Press, 1999), 431.

2. Summers, *J. Edgar Hoover: Official and Confidential*, Chapter 33.

3. Kennealy, *Strange Days*, 152.

4. Interview reproduced on *The Ultimate Spoken Word Collection,* compact disc.

5. Ashcroft, *Wild Child*, 469. In her account, Ashcroft claims Jim showed her this astonishing letter. Although it does not appear on Jim's file, it could be one of the three pages that remain withheld or alternatively part of Hoover's Official and Confidential correspondence file (which was destroyed soon after his death). In fact, there would be no reason to keep an FBI record of the letter at all. Since Ashcroft's book seems accurate, I have little reason to doubt her.

6. Ibid., 386.

7. That would have been a catastrophic move. The Establishment knew Kennealy helped with Democrat Bobby Kennedy's 1968 New York campaign. Besides, she never went to the Dinner Key show.

8. Interview reproduced on *The Ultimate Spoken Word Collection,* compact disc.

9. Mailer, *Miami and the Siege of Chicago*, 35.

10. Riordan and Prochnicky, *Break on Through*, 166.

11. Kennealy, *Strange Days*, 47.

12. Ibid., 331.

Chapter 11: THIRD MAN

1. Interview reproduced on *The Ultimate Spoken Word Collection,* compact disc.

2. He told journalists the same thing; see Riordan and Prochnicky, *Break on Through*, 394.

3. Interview reproduced on *The Ultimate Spoken Word Collection,* compact disc.

4. Murray Goodman might have added that people who went to *Hair* knew what to expect. Teens coming to see the Doors (whose singles rode high in the pop charts) did not - and the Orange Bowl registered their dismay. But some of the same kids demanded groups as far out as Jefferson Airplane. Goodman disallowed many Doors witness statements; for him the youth of Miami were incapable of deciding their own standard of decency.

5. Interview reproduced on *The Ultimate Spoken Word Collection,* compact disc.

6. Ibid.

7. Kennealy, *Strange Days*, 210.

8. Goodman had no interest in reaching an acquittal or light sentence for such a high profile case, especially as his re-election was due on September 8th. Everybody knew it. Last time, Robert

Josefsberg (The Doors' Miami lawyer) was offered the same position and turned it down. Evidence suggests they postponed the re-election until November - just after Judge Goodman had sentenced Jim.

9. See Riordan and Prochnicky, *Break on Through*, 394.

10. Interview reproduced on *The Ultimate Spoken Word Collection,* compact disc.

11. Patricia Butler mentions Jim's meeting with Meyer's girl at the Fontainebleau. See Butler, *The Tragic Romance of Pamela & Jim Morrison,* 150.

Chapter 12: THE END

1. Reproduced in Riordan and Prochnicky, *Break on Through*, 412.

2. Interview reproduced on *The Ultimate Spoken Word Collection,* compact disc.

3. Ibid.

4. Ibid.

5. Riordan and Prochnicky, *Break on Through*, 417.

6. Ibid., 315.

7. Interview reproduced on *The Ultimate Spoken Word Collection,* compact disc.

8. Ibid.

9. Ashcroft, *Wild Child*, 445.

10. Kennealy, *Strange Days*, 257.

11. Ibid., 316.

Chapter 13: INTERESTED IN FREEDOM

1. Manzarek, *Light My Fire*, 2.

2. Drug information from: Canadian Department of Health and Welfare, *Bad Trips, Freakouts, Overdoses: Emergency Treatment of Drug Crises* (Ottawa: Information Canada, 1975), 29.

3. Beck and Malina, "Paradise Now," *Tulane Drama Review.*

4. Crist, quoted in Gary Fineout, "Jim Morrison is Pardoned in

Indecent Exposure Case," *New York Times*, December 9, 2010, available:

http://artsbeat.blogs.nytimes.com/2010/12/09/jim-morrison-is-pardoned-in-indecent-exposure-case/

5. Jim ended a letter to Dave Marsh at *Creem* with this phrase. Reproduced in Hopkins and Sugarman, *No One Gets Out of Here Alive*, 343.

Jim Morrison
1969 – 1971
Chronology / Discography

1969

Early February: ***Wishful Sinful*** single released. Jim Morrison arrested in LA for driving drunk and without a license. He also makes out a will to Pamela Courson.

February 24-28: Morrison attends the Living Theatre's USC shows. *Rock is Dead* session *may* have taken place at this time.

March 1: The Doors' infamous Dinner Key concert in Miami.

March 3: Larry Mahoney's pivotal *Miami Herald* story, 'Rock Group Fails To Stir A Riot.'

Chapter 4

March 4: Special Agent Whittaker's Miami FBI report mentions the Dinner Key event.

March 5: City of Miami swear out a warrant for the arrest of Jim Morrison.

March 9: Morrison makes a private donation of $2,500 to the Living Theatre.

March 20: Charles Crutchfield writes a complaint about a Fugs album and a Morrison news clipping. He sends his letter to J. Edgar Hoover.

March 23: Orange Bowl Rally for Decency in Miami.

March 26: Orange Bowl Rally organizer Mike Levesque receives a letter from President Nixon. Hoover responds to Crutchfield's enquiry.

March 27: US Commissioner Ed Swan swears out a city of Miami fugitive warrant for the arrest of Jim Morrison.

April 3: Morrison 'surrenders' to agents in the FBI's LA field office.

Mid April: Jim Morrison and friends film *HWY* near Palm Springs.

April 18: Governor Claude Kirk signs Morrison's Florida fugitive warrant.

April 23: Kirk's office issues Morrison's official Florida fugitive warrant.

April 24: US Attorney Michael Osman closes the fugitive case.

May: ***Tell All The People*** single released. Doors perform on public television for WNET in New York. Morrison reads *American Prayer* at a benefit in LA for Norman Mailer's campaign to become mayor of New York.

June 28 - July 1: The Doors play Mexico City.

July: ***Soft Parade*** album released. It reaches no. 6 in the US album charts.

July 21: Doors play two shows in LA's Aquarius Theatre for the ***Absolutely Live*** album.

July 27: Doors join other top bands at the Seattle Pop Festival.

August: ***Runnin' Blue*** single released, but does poorly in charts. Jay Sebring murdered.

September 13: Doors share bill with John Lennon at Toronto's Rock'n'roll Revival show.

November 9: Morrison returns to Miami to enter his plea of "Not guilty."

November 11: Tom Baker and Jim Morrison arrested off Flight 172 to Phoenix.

November 12: Baker and Morrison charged by city police for public drunkenness, and by a US Marshal for the intimidation of a flight crew.

November 20: The FBI receive a UPI press release about the Phoenix incident. Late in November The Doors begin to record ***Morrison Hotel*** at Sunset Sound studios.

November 24: Morrison and Baker miss their initial Phoenix hearing.

December 9: Jim has nervous breakdown at the Doors' office on Santa Monica Boulevard.

December 12: Morrison and Baker plead 'not guilty' in a Phoenix courtroom.

December 16: FBI agents inform the FAA about Morrison's behaviour on Flight 172.

1970

January 17-18: The Doors play the Felt Forum in New York's Madison Square Garden. Part of the show eventually appears on *The Doors Box Set.*

January 20: The FBI in Phoenix send Hoover a reminder: Jim's trial there is approaching.

February: ***Morrison Hotel*** is released. It reaches no.4 in the US and no.12 in UK charts.

March: ***You Make Me Real / Roadhouse Blues*** single released.

March 3: Superseding indictment presented against Morrison and Baker in Phoenix.

March 12: Local FBI agents inform Hoover of Morrison's new Phoenix trial date.

March 26: Morrison found guilty by Judge Copple in Phoenix. He faces three months in jail plus a $300 fine.

April 1: Lawyer Max Fink requests postponement of the

Phoenix sentence.

April 15: Max Fink files to present a new motion in the Phoenix case.

April 20: Jim Morrison is acquitted in Phoenix on the grounds of mistaken identity. The FBI then inform the FAA, who threaten Morrison with a $2000 civil suit.

April: Publication of *The Lords and the New Creatures* by James Douglas Morrison.

May 4: Four students shot dead by National Guardsmen at Kent State.

June 24: Jim Morrison hand-fasts with Patricia Kennealy. He pays FAA $600 that month.

July: ***Absolutely Live*** album released and reaches no. 8 in the US album charts.

August 6: Morrison arrested for public drunkenness after falling asleep on an LA doorstep.

August 7: Jim Morrison flies to Miami ready for his trial.

August 10: Jury selection begins for the Miami trial.

August 14: Jury sworn in, ready for Morrison's trial.

August 17: The trial begins in Miami.

August 21-22: The Doors are released from Florida to play in Bakersfield and San Diego.

August 29: Exhausted, the Doors make a rapid visit to play the Isle of Wight Festival.

Chapter 4

September 20: Morrison found guilty on *some* counts by a jury in Miami. His lawyers begin an appeal.

October 30: Miami's Judge Goodman sentences Morrison for his Dinner Key antics. He gets a $500 fine and six months of hard labour (plus a sixty day concurrent sentence).

December 8: Jim records poetry on his birthday in Village Recorders studio. The tapes are eventually used to create ***An American Prayer***.

December 12: Morrison's last live performance with the Doors, at the Warehouse in New Orleans.

1971

March: ***Love Her Madly*** single released. Jim leaves LA for Paris.

April: ***LA Woman*** album released and reaches no. 5 on the US album charts.

June: ***Riders on the Storm / The Changeling*** single released.

July 3: Jim Morrison is found dead in Paris.

July 7: Jim's body is buried in Père-Lachaise cemetery.

Recommended Reading and References

Artaud, A. 1965. *Anthology*. San Francisco: City Lights Books.

Artaud, A. 1970. *The Theatre and Its Double*. London: Calder and Boyars.

Ashcroft, L. 1997. *Wild Child: Life With Jim Morrison*. New York: Da Capo Press.

Butler, P. 2007. *The Tragic Romance of Pamela & Jim Morrison*. London: Omnibus Press.

Recommended Reading

Clarke, R. 1993. *The Doors: Dance on Fire*. Chessington: Castle / Penguin.

Crisafulli, C. 2000. *The Doors: When The Music's Over*. New York: Da Capo Press.

de Tocquville, A. 1990. *Democracy in America*. New York: Vintage Books.

Densmore, J. 1991. *Riders On The Storm*. London: Bloomsbury.

Fowlie, W. 1994. *Rimbaud and Jim Morrison: The Rebel as Poet*. Durham: Duke University Press.

Hoover, J.E. 1961. *Masters of Deceit: The Story of Communism in America and How to Fight It*. Pocket Books: New York.

Hopkins, J. and Sugerman, D. 1995. *No One Gets Out of Here Alive*. New York: Warner Books.

Hopkins, J. 1995. *The Lizard King: The Essential Jim Morrison*. New York: Fireside.

Huddleston, J. 1991. *This is the End My Only Friend*. New York: Shapolsky Publishers.

Kennealy-Morrison, P. 1998. *Strange Days: My Life With and Without Jim Morrison*. London: Harper Collins.

Lipton, L. 1959. *The Holy Barbarians*. New York: Messner.

Lisciandro, F. 1993. *Jim Morrison: An Hour for the Magic*. London: Plexus.

Mailer, N. 2008. *Miami and The Siege of Chicago: An Informal History of the American Political Conventions of 1968*. New York: NYRB Classics.

Malina, J. 1972. *The Enormous Despair*. New York: Random House.

Manzarek, R. 1998. *Light My Fire: My Life with the Doors*. New York: Berkley Boulevard.

Marcus, G. 2011. *The Doors: A Lifetime of Listening to Five Mean Years*. London: Faber and Faber.

Morrison, J. 1988. *Wilderness: The Lost Writings of Jim Morrison Volume I*. New York: Vintage Books.

Morrison, J. 1991. *The American Night: The Writings of Jim Morrison Volume II*. New York: Vintage Books.

Riordan, J. and Prochnicky, J. 1992. *Break on Through: The Life and Death of Jim Morrison*. New York: It Books.

Recommended Reading

Rostagno A. with Beck, J. and Malina, J. 1970. *We: The Living Theatre*. New York: Ballantine Books.

Sugerman, D. 1988. *The Doors: The Illustrated History*. Omnibus Press: London.

Summers, A. 1993. *Official and Confidential: The Secret Life of J. Edgar Hoover*. New York: Putnam Adult.

Turner, W. 1970. *Hoover's FBI: The Men and The Myth*. Los Angeles: Sherbourne Press.

Weidman, R. 2011. *The Doors FAQ: All That's Left to Know About the Kings of Acid Rock*. Milwaukee: Backbeat Books.

www.ingramcontent.com/pod-product-compliance
Lightning Source LLC
LaVergne TN
LVHW051124080426
835510LV00018B/2219

* 9 7 8 0 9 5 7 0 5 1 1 8 8 *